No. 12 Kaiserhofstrasse

No. 12
Kaiserhofstrasse

Valentin Senger

Translated by Ralph Manheim

E. P. Dutton | New York

For information contact:
E. P. Dutton, 2 Park Avenue, New York, N.Y. 10016

Library of Congress Cataloging in Publication Data
Senger, Valentin.
No. 12 Kaiserhofstrasse.
Translation of Kaiserhofstrasse 12.
1. Senger, Valentin. 2. Jews in Frankfurt am Main—Biography.
3. Jews in Germany—History—1933–1945.
4. Frankfurt am Main—Biography. I. Title.
DS135.G5S46713   943'.41 [B]   79–15084
ISBN: 0-525-13816-1

Published simultaneously in Canada by
Clarke, Irwin & Company Limited, Toronto and Vancouver

Designed by Dorothy Schmiderer

10 9 8 7 6 5 4 3 2 1

First Edition

Contents

Amtliches Frankf

Adreßbuchverlag Scherl

Arrow indicates Kaiserhofstrasse. Other Nazi names include Horst Wessel Platz (formerly Rathenau

r Adreßbuch 1939

"Official Frankfurt Street Directory, 1939."

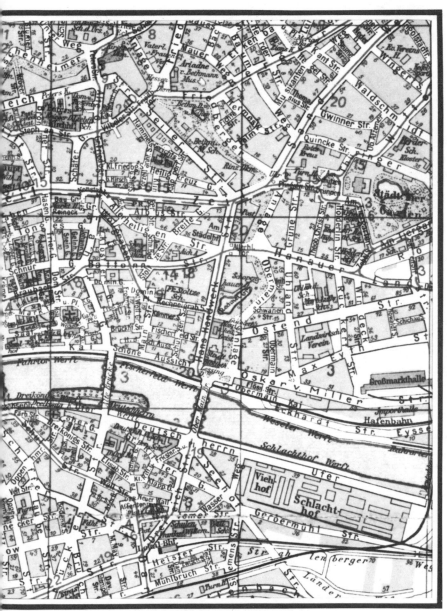

Platz), Adolf Hitler Anlage, Speicher Strasse, Hermann Göring Ufer.

Mama

In my earliest childhood memory I see myself under a round table, playing with a tin clown who is driving a donkey cart and brandishing a whip. There are legs all around me, some in trousers, some in silk stockings. One pair of the legs in silk stockings belongs to Mama. When I venture too far out from under the table with my donkey cart, somebody pulls in his legs, and I remember the sound of feet shuffling over the wooden floor. Now and then someone pats me on the head; that's supposed to be a sign of affection. Beside me on the floor there's another toy, a green snake made of inch-long joints of wood. When I pick up the snake by the tail, it wriggles as if it were alive and even sticks out its tongue. Overhead the talk goes on and on.

The legs enclose me like the bars of a cage. The voices are loud; sometimes—to judge by the sound, at least—they seem to be fighting. Mama does most of the talking; her clear voice rises above the others. Though I hear that voice all day long, it sounds strange to me today, different than usual. And

Mama's laugh sounds different too. She's right here, I could easily touch her legs, and yet she's far away, and this impression is accentuated by the thin-rimmed pince-nez she wears on such occasions. She never wears it while doing housework or reading the paper. After they've all sat down, she grasps it between thumb and forefinger (while delicately arching her other three fingers), removes it from its black-enameled tin case, opens it out and carefully sets it on her nose. The pince-nez stands like a wall between her and me.

As far back as I can remember, Mama was always busy. Her working day had sixteen hours, her working week seven days. In addition to keeping house unaided for a family of five, she made every stitch of the clothing we children wore. But her hand-sewn garments were only practical, never becoming; they took future growth into account and never quite fitted; the coats were too thick, the knee-length trousers too long, the shirts too bulky. Thanks to her clothes, we were a laughing-stock in our street and outsiders at school. Once she made me a knapsack for country outings out of a brown oilcloth shopping bag, and all that summer the other children called me "Hunch-bag." She sewed for other people too. She washed our clothes and our roomer's as well. He was a Jewish traveling salesman; supposedly she was taking his soiled clothing to the laundry and to keep him from noticing her little dodge, my sister, Paula, had to make out fake bills from the laundry. This went on for years. He pretended not to notice, but Paula, who always brought him the bills with his clean washing, knew he was only pretending. Mama hung wallpaper, painted doors and ceilings, and upholstered the sofa. And as if that were not enough, she occasionally interpreted in court and did translations from Russian into German.

If someone were to ask me now how she managed to do all that, I could only turn my palms upward in the classical Jewish gesture, and say: All I know is that she did it. I couldn't say how, though I watched her day after day. If she put one piece of work down, it was only to pick up another; she never rested, never took an afternoon nap, or stopped for a cup of coffee. When acute heart trouble finally forced her to spend all of her time in bed, she could hardly bear it.

Mama couldn't help driving herself; you'd have thought she was deliberately trying to drive herself into the ground. She'd get angry if anyone tried to make her stop, if Papa told her to sit down and rest a few minutes. "A *chachem!*"* she'd say. "That's what you are. Who's going to do the work if I don't? You, I suppose?" Papa had no answer to that, and she was at it harder than ever.

As if the housework and all this running around weren't enough for her, she was active in several political organizations. She was on the executive committees of the left-leaning Jewish Workers' Cultural Society, of the Anti-Imperialist League and of an action committee for the Abolition of Paragraph 218, the anti-abortion law. She worked for the Red Aid and the International Workers' Aid, both close to the Communist Party, of which she was also a member. She attended meetings almost every night, and her comrades often came to our apartment; they came and went as they pleased at any hour of the day and sometimes in the middle of the night. Our apartment was a clearinghouse for news, a place where overworked party functionaries could meet and talk.

Papa was at the factory all day and came home exhausted. After work Paula and I would meet him at the streetcar stop. He'd always have a few candies for us or a bit of chocolate, and on Friday, which was payday, he sometimes had a whole bar of chocolate or some toy he had bought from one of the peddlers who did a thriving business that day outside the factory gates. He could be very witty when he had had enough sleep, which only happened on Sunday. He had an inexhaustible stock of Russian and Yiddish sayings, and he rarely made

Chachem—"wise man," here with the implication of "wise guy."

a statement without throwing one in. If someone asked a question, he'd often answer with an appropriate proverb. That made a big impression on me. Another of his Yiddish mannerisms was to answer a question with a question such as "Why should I?" and "Why shouldn't I?"

Much as I loved him, I could never forgive him for being more of a grandfather than a father to me. He was forty-eight when I was born, and as far back as I can remember he had the stooped shoulders of a tired ghetto Jew. His bent back seemed to express all the tragedy of Jewish existence. He was too old to run and jump with me, too old to be an understanding friend; he could only be good and kind.

There were three children: Paula was nearly two years older than me and Alex was five years younger. Mama would have cut herself to pieces for us if necessary, but since she was cutting herself to pieces for a dozen other things, she didn't have much time for us, and didn't really like us to bother her.

*

All your life, Mama, you knocked yourself out for us, your family, and for others, your political friends. You sacrificed yourself. The heart trouble that killed you was the price you paid for it. If there's a God and if he's just, I'll bet he threw his arms around you and hugged you long and hard. All through my childhood I wished you'd hug me that way. But you never had time to, you were busy with other things.

I can still feel Papa's kisses, his lips, his beard; I remember the way he hugged me. But, Mama, I don't feel your kisses. All I remember is the nasty smell when you pulled one corner of a handkerchief over your finger and spat on it before wiping my nose or mouth. Did you ever kiss me? I don't remember.

The Revolutionary

In December 1905 Moissey Rabizanovich, the son of a whole-
sale grain merchant and himself a skilled metal worker, fled
from Russia with the Okhrana, the czarist secret police, hot on
his heels. Moissey came of an Orthodox Jewish family. Up to
that time—he was then thirty-five—his life had been extremely turbulent. At Odessa University, where he was studying engineering, he belonged to an illegal revolutionary cell.
After five or six terms, convinced that political agitation with
a view to overthrowing the Czar was more important than
study, he left the university and went to work in a locomotive
factory. Some years later he was discharged for revolutionary
activity, arrested, tried, and sentenced to a year in a dilapidated
old fortress near Odessa, where he contracted a lung ailment
that plagued him to the end of his life. Once—and this was
his most tormenting memory—he was flogged before the as-
sembled inmates for participating in a protest against the bad
food. On his release he found work in a French steel mill near
Odessa, where, after twelve workers had been killed in an

accident, he and a few others organized the first strike. This
was around the turn of the century.

At the age of twenty-seven he married seventeen-year-old
Olga Sudakovich despite the opposition of her wealthy parents,
who owned a Black Sea fishing fleet and a canning factory. Her
father called him a *bosnyak,* a ne'er-do-well, who would never
be able to support a family; her mother's objection was that he
had given up the Jewish religion, that he ate *trayf,* * didn't keep
the Sabbath, and never set foot in a synagogue. In spite of her
father's curses and her mother's tears, Olga followed Moissey
to Odessa, though she took little interest in politics and was
certainly no revolutionary. She was in Odessa when the revolution of 1905 broke out and spread through the industrial cities
of the Ukraine. Moissey played a leading role and when the
revolution was crushed at the end of the year he went underground.

Olga lived in a wretched apartment on the outskirts and
trembled for her husband. She had never imagined that her
married life would be like this. Only now did she realize that
most of her days and nights would be spent without a husband,
and that for the present there could be no thought of having
children. "I can't take the responsibility for having children
when there's every chance they'd grow up without a father,"
Moissey would say. "How do I know what will happen to me
today or tomorrow?"

His name was on all the wanted lists. In an adventure-
filled flight, he crossed the Ukraine and White Russia, making
his way through Moscow and Warsaw, and from there political
friends helped him to cross the German border. In March 1906
he arrived in Berlin.

That Russian refugee, Moissey Rabizanovich, was my father.

This is Papa's story of his escape from czarist Russia,
that's how he told it to me. Mama's version is entirely different,

---

Trayf—"unclean" food, forbidden by the dietary laws. The opposite of *kosher.*

no revolutionary heroism about it. According to her, Papa left Russia to keep out of the army. Jews were conscripted for the first time during the Russo-Japanese War of 1904–5. For the first time Russian Jews were considered worthy to bear arms. But sooner than let themselves be shot dead for the Czar, a good many left the country. And that was how Papa came to Berlin.

I'm inclined to believe Papa's version. Not because it's more exciting; there are other reasons. Papa was a reticent man, never one to boast; he preferred saying too little rather than too much. And one day, when with some difficulty I got him to talk about his life in Russia, there was no trace of heroics in his story; it was simply a matter-of-fact account of events which he now saw as history and in which he himself had played a subordinate role.

It was only by repeated questioning that I found out, for instance, that he had been a member of a workers' committee that had met with a delegation from the crew of the cruiser *Potemkin,* or that he had several times been sent as a courier to Sebastopol, the home port of the Black Sea fleet, or that he had helped to found *Borba (Struggle)* the first illegal Bolshevik newspaper. His story was too full of personal details for him to have made it up. But my main reason for doubting Mama's version is that she did a brilliant job of covering up their past, for fear it might make trouble for the family at some future date. She spread a dense layer of lies over their former life. Some instinct seems to have told her that our very survival depended on it.

The Russian refugee community in Berlin took Papa under its wing. During the first few months he worked exclusively for the Bolsheviks; he had become a professional revolutionary.

A year later, in the spring of 1907, Mama joined him in Berlin. But even there she didn't see much more of her husband than she had in Odessa. He was absent a good deal, and late that summer, as Mama told me, he suddenly vanished from Berlin; she never found out exactly why. He was gone for two years. Where he was all that time and what he had been doing, he never told us. That left room for all sorts of speculation: buying armaments for the Russian revolutionaries, planting bombs, carrying secret messages, spying. But it may have been something much more inoffensive.

He did tell us, though, that he'd been in Switzerland several times, and he was proud of having met Lenin and his wife, Krupskaya, in Geneva. He saw other Russian revolutionaries in Geneva, as well, but I was never able to find out any more about his dealings with them, any more than the reason for his mysterious disappearance.

In 1909 my father came back to Berlin from Switzerland with a forged Russian passport. His name was now Jakob Senger, and his wife's maiden name had become Fuhrmann. The new passport and new name marked a turning point in his life. He cast off his revolutionary past, became a respectable citizen with a legal identity, registered with the police, rented an apartment on Schönhauser Allee, and took a job as a lathe operator in an elevator factory. He was then thirty-nine.

In 1911 my parents moved to Offenbach and a few months later to Frankfurt, where my father found work as a turret lathe operator at the Adler Plant. But he lived in fear that his revolutionary past would catch up with him and that he and Mama would be deported. What if the police discovered that his passport was false? And perhaps the worst danger of all—his accent? For he never learned to speak German properly; his German still sounded like Yiddish, and continued to do so throughout the Hitler period.

The Cover-Up

The move to Frankfurt marked the beginning of Mama's cover-up maneuvers, of her desperate efforts to wipe out the past, or at least to muddy the traces so completely that no one would ever be able to track them down. The move to Frankfurt was the first step. Before leaving Offenbach, Mama worked out an elaborate plan. Instead of going directly to Frankfurt, they informed the police that they were leaving for Zurich, which indeed they did. In Zurich Papa registered with the police and obtained a residence permit. Two weeks later he went back to the police and obtained a certificate of departure. This, on his arrival, he presented to the Frankfurt police, who noted on his new registration: "Previous residence: Zurich."

The more Papa settled down, the more active Mama became. Papa seemed tired. The ends of his mustache, which had formerly twirled upward, now drooped down over the corners of his mouth and he began to walk with a shuffle. At the same time Mama, ceasing to be the traditional self-effacing Jewish wife, took firm control of our home; from then on it was she who made the decisions. This change in roles took place without a word; Papa put up no resistance, he didn't seem to want it any other way. Mama also took charge of the family planning. In 1917, after they had been married for twenty years, my sister, Paula, was born; I came along in 1918 and my brother, Alex, in 1923.

Despite all her precautions, one thing Mama never dreamed of was that in a liberal, cosmopolitan city like Frankfurt, where Jews and Christians had been living side by side for centuries, the mere fact of being a Jew could ever become a mortal danger. It didn't worry her that the police had put our religion down as "Hebraic."

In spite of Papa's revolutionary past, my parents always thought of themselves as Jews. However, they belonged to the Jewish community only in the most formal sense and had little contact with its members. All that remained of the Jewish homes they had known in childhood was a few nostalgic memories: a Jewish Momma, the sheltered feeling that comes of a large family, a pious father who before the Sabbath meal chanted the *Kiddush*, or blessing, over a glass of wine and broke the bread with a prayer; Purim, the feast of Esther, when the children's rejoicing sometimes takes rather riotous forms, the marriage ceremony performed under a *chuppa*, or canopy, in accordance with Mosaic law.

Papa often took me to the Reform synagogue on Freiherr-vom-Stein Strasse. Before I left the house, Mama covered my head with a beret, which served exclusively for my visits to the synagogue. Papa put on his black felt hat, which was likewise reserved for synagogue use and spent the rest of the time in a cloth case on the top shelf of the wardrobe. We went mostly on the Jewish holidays and always, it goes without saying, on Yom Kippur. This visit to the synagogue on the holiest of all Jewish holidays, when a Jew repents all his transgressions of the past year, spends the whole day in prayer, and at nightfall stands immaculate before his Maker, meant a great deal to me. As we left the house, Papa took my hand, something he seldom did, and held on to it the whole way. He explained the meaning of Rosh Hashanah, the Jewish New Year, of Yom Kippur, the Day of Atonement, and of the intervening ten days of repentance, and told me how these High Holidays had been celebrated at home in Russia. Then he'd come back to the Day of Atonement; of course it was foolish, he said, to imagine that by repenting for one day a man could wipe out all the sins he had committed on the previous three hundred and sixty-four. That was all wrong, Papa thought, and I couldn't help agreeing with him.

Anyway, most Jews, even if they're not religious, go to the synagogue on Yom Kippur to repent the sins of the past year. For this they are well rewarded; the year's transgressions, for which they would otherwise be called to account in the next world, are expunged from God's big ledger. If a Jew does not repent before sunset, when the book is closed, the record of his sins will stand fast for another year.

No wonder the synagogues are full to bursting, said Papa. Who would miss this golden opportunity to wipe out a whole year's transgressions by a few hours of repentance and prayer? He doubted that God could be so unreasonable, but he wasn't quite sure, and that was why he took me to the Yom Kippur services every year. Sometimes we even went on Erev Yom Kippur, the previous evening when the holiday actually begins and the *Kol Nidre* is sung.

I would stand wedged into the praying crowd somewhere at the back of the synagogue—Papa and I always remained standing. All I could see were the black coats of the men in front of me; Papa stood behind me, with his hands on my shoulders. I heard the monotonous singsong of the congregation and now and then the lone voice of the cantor. I noticed how the rhythmic movements of the men at the center, whom I could not see, surged back to the last rows of the standing congregants. Though I didn't understand a word of the prayers, and though we stayed there for several hours, I was never bored for a single minute. I succumbed to the spell of communal prayer.

And since Yom Kippur is a day of reconciliation, not only

with God but also with our fellow men, there was an endless shaking of hands and exchanging of good wishes, first on the way to the synagogue and then in earnest on the way home. On that day we all wished each other well. Shalom, forgive and forget. We children turned it into a game and played at reconciliation.

I sensed that it wasn't just to humor their Jewish friends that my parents joined in this ritual. No, almost in spite of themselves they were drawn back into the Jewish tradition. Before and after the day Papa told all sorts of jokes and stories to show that he didn't set much store by these religious observances, which only served to stress their ties with Judaism.

Sometimes when Mama sat at her sewing machine, making a blouse or a dress for strangers, she would call me over to her and tell me something about the history of the Jewish people, for instance, about how Esther and Mordecai had saved the Persian Jews, or how the Zealots had fought the Romans. Or she'd reminisce about her family in Russia. It was she, not Papa, who told me one day that the Rabizanoviches were *Kohanim,* * and could boast some of the most famous rabbis in southern Russia. My father's father, it seems, had studied to be a rabbi, but Mama didn't tell me why he had become a grain merchant instead.

I gathered from little hints dropped by my father that my grandfather—whom I never knew—was far from averse to the pleasures of the flesh. He was an imposing-looking man (as I could see from a daguerreotype they had managed to save) and he liked to spend money. At the rabbinic academy he had been drawn far more to women and idleness than to study, and that was why he was never privileged to become the spiritual leader of a Jewish congregation.

Mama said it was an honor to belong to a family of *Kohanim.* I was glad to hear that; it comforted me a little for

---

*Kohen—priest. Jews bearing the name of Kohen are supposedly descended from the sons of Aaron.

the drabness of our present surroundings. Papa didn't share my enthusiasm. He only winked and said that Jews collected *Kohanim* the way Christians collected relics of Christ and the saints.

Circumcision

Papa, too, did his best to bring us up in the Jewish tradition. In addition to taking me to the synagogue and telling me about Jewish customs and beliefs, he taught me the Hebrew alphabet and the Hannukah song. And one day he took me to the Jewish graveyard. That meant a lot to me because I had no relatives in Germany and therefore we had never had a death in the family. So I didn't know how Jews mourned and remembered their dead. I've never in all my life known a grandfather or grandmother, an uncle, aunt, or cousin; they had all stayed in Russia or emigrated to other countries. This may have seriously impaired the emotional development of us children, because it's the extended Jewish family, with its bustle and confusion from morning to night, the special excitement every week before the Sabbath, the exaggerated fussing over the children and respect for the old people, that give so many Jews their feeling of being at home in the world.

The only relative I ever got to know was Mama's niece, Taya Baumstein. She lived with us for a year or two while studying music at the Hoch Conservatory in Frankfurt. She was extremely beautiful, I remember, and full of life, and men turned to look at her in the street. Then she got married and went to live in Toulouse with her husband. I saw her again in 1937 when she helped me to get a French visa—and then again at the beginning of 1946 at Höchenschwand in the Black Forest, in the French-occupied zone of Germany, where she had gone for a cure. In the meantime horrible things had happened. Her husband—fellow inmates told her later—had been murdered by drowning in Buchenwald, and she herself had spent three years in the Ravensbrück concentration camp, where SS doctors had performed medical experiments on her legs. She could hardly walk, and then only with a cane, and when she lifted her trouser legs, I saw that her legs were still covered with scars and festering sores. Big chunks had been hacked out of her calves. She committed suicide a few months later.

I'll never forget the time Papa took me down the rows of graves in the old Jewish graveyard on Rat-Beil Strasse, showed me the symbols on the tombstones, and explained why there were pebbles lying on many of the graves. We sat down on a wall and Papa told me how the Jews—unlike most Christians —were required by custom to bury the dead in plain wooden coffins as quickly and simply as possible and how the family had to "sit *shivah*" for seven days, meaning to sit at home without shoes on low stools, receiving condolence calls. But after sitting *shivah*, (even though the dead were mourned for thirty days more and indeed for a whole year in the case of a father or mother) the mourners were expected to turn back to the concerns of earthly life. They were supposed to let the dead rest in peace and give the wounds of the living a chance to heal. That was why Jews go so seldom to cemeteries, although they believe in a life after death in which the righteous will be richly rewarded and the sinners get their just punishment. I'm not sure Papa believed in a hereafter, but judging by everything he told me, I imagine he did.

A week after my brother, Alex, was born, we had a big celebration. Papa stayed home from work. First thing in the morning he swept and cleaned the whole apartment. Though Mama was already up and about, making herself as busy as ever, Papa did all the cleaning by himself that morning. Mama's job was to sit on the sofa the whole time, at most looking after the new baby, giving him her breast and changing him. Alex was wearing a beautiful little woolen jacket. My sister, Paula, and I both had to put on our best clothes, shine our shoes, and wash our hands, and Mama and Papa were all dressed up too.

Then the big moment came; the *mohel*, or circumciser, arrived, punctual and walking at a measured pace, looking very solemn and self-important in his black caftan and stiff black hat. He was followed by a young assistant, carrying the tools of the trade in a worn leather case. In the big back room, our parents' bedroom, Mama laid little Alex down on the bed closest to the window, so as to give the *mohel* plenty of light. The baby was already yelling bloody murder as if he suspected what was coming. She set him down on a quilted silk coverlet and took off his diapers. Mindful of his clients' property, the *mohel* began by placing a square of linen between the baby's behind and the silk coverlet. Then he said a prayer. So as not to get in the *mohel*'s way, the onlookers—a few friends of the family, my sister, and me in my beret—had to stand on the other side of the beds. Only Mama and Papa stood close by. Papa was wearing his black felt hat. The assistant handed the *mohel* the instruments, and the *mohel*, who kept his jacket on but turned up his sleeves, set to work.

Poor little Alex let out a bloodcurdling scream as his little foreskin was cut off. I was still very small, so I didn't get a good view of the proceedings. It all went very quickly. When it was over, Alex was bandaged up, and then the *mohel* said a longer prayer. Then Mama and Papa laid their hands on little Alex's head and blessed him.

To me the whole ceremony was very exciting and, though

more than fifty years have passed since then, I can still remember many details: the assistant's face with its acne or chickenpox scars, the black case with the scalpel, and a tin powder box shaped like a pagoda, which the *mohel* set down on the marble top of the dressing table. And I also remember Mama's pouring water over the *mohel's* hands from the china pitcher with the blue flower pattern.

Mama put a rubber nipple dipped in honey in Alex's mouth to quiet him, the *mohel* drank a glass of wine with Papa —his assistant did not partake—and they went into the next room to settle the business end. Then after a while the *mohel* and his assistant left.

Later Mama said to me, "Did you see it, Valya? It was just the same with you." It gave me the shivers to think of it.

That evening the event was celebrated with a big bowl of borsht, quantities of meat and fish, several desserts, and mountains of cakes. Everything had been got ready the day before. There were bottles and bottles of wine and the samovar was kept humming all afternoon and night. Papa never drank much wine, but on a day like that he'd take ten or fifteen cups of tea. More and more guests kept coming, each with a little present for Alex. I'd seldom seen Mama and Papa so happy and lively. A young woman helped Papa to wait on the guests. Mama sat on the divan, drank kosher wine, and talked politics with the guests, most of whom were political friends who had come to help us celebrate the event. Now and then Papa would tell one of his stories.

When Paula and I were sent to bed, the party was still at its height. The people were all laughing and singing Russian and Yiddish songs; it went on and on, and there was so much noise it took us a long time to get to sleep.

Our Street

When I started writing this book, my idea was to tell the story of my family and how we miraculously survived the Hitler years, and that is still my purpose. Though properly it should start in 1933, I see that my thoughts keep carrying me further and further back. It's as if my memories had started a heavy flywheel, and once it's in motion, it's not so easy to stop. But come to think of it, it's just as well, because a good deal of what happened to my parents, my brother, and my sister in the Nazi period would be hard to understand without some knowledge of our earlier life in Frankfurt.

From 1917 on, my parents lived in a house at the back of the house at No. 12 Kaiserhofstrasse, a short street (the numbers stopped at 20) between Hauptwache and Opernplatz. And that's where I was born. Kaiserhofstrasse connected Hochstrasse with the almost parallel Fressgasse.* The real name was Grosse Bockenheimerstrasse, but everybody called it

*Fressgasse—"Swill Street." Fressen—to eat, gobble, swill.

Fressgasse. A lot of people didn't even know its right name. Rollenhagen, the fanciest delicatessen in Frankfurt, was located on Fressgasse. Many a day I'd flatten my nose against the plate glass windows and stare at the artfully displayed delicacies, most of which I didn't even know by name, and at the rich ladies and gentlemen inside, who could afford such luxuries. I'd stare until my breath fogged up the glass.

But Rollenhagen was only one of the many shops that had given Fressgasse its name. There was Petri's cheese emporium at the corner of Kaiserhofstrasse, with its gigantic wheels of Swiss cheeses, cut in half, piled up in pyramids; there was Kremser's fish market, the whole front of which was one enormous aquarium with fish from all the seven seas swimming around in it; there was the luxurious Wörner-Simmer confectionery, which I couldn't pass without dreaming of the day when, as I fervently hoped, I would taste one of those sumptuously displayed assorted chocolates; there was Plöger's delicatessen, which in those days was much smaller than Rollenhagen's but is still in existence today, whereas Rollenhagen's failed soon after the Second World War, which shows the dangers of overexpansion. There was Weinschrod's fruit store, which I detested because I was always being sent there for ten pfennigs' worth of bruised fruit; I also hated Emmerich's butcher shop, because who wants to shop for "twenty pfennigs' worth of bologna ends"? Also fresh in my memory are Fritz Lochner, the baker, who became famous far beyond the city limits, and that astute butcher Stephan Weiss, who, just before the dirigible *Graf Zeppelin* was due to land for the first time in Frankfurt, invented a new sausage mixture, crammed it into a skin a yard long and three inches thick, and donated his giant sausage to the crew of the *Zeppelin,* whereupon he was authorized to call his creation "Zeppelin sausage" forever after. I have no doubt that he has sold miles and miles of it by now.

Back to Kaiserhofstrasse. Short as it was, it seems to have been a rather high-class street. But alas, only the front buildings could claim that distinction, and we lived in the back—Papa was a manual worker. Anyway, our street was higher class than the two streets parallel to it on either side, Meisengasse and Kleine Hochstrasse, which were about the same length.

The houses on our street dated from the 1870's, the prosperous first years of the German Empire. Most of them had imposing, well-kept red sandstone façades with balustrades, window niches, and other ornamental features. The tenants were civil servants, artisans, and small businessmen. Even some of the owners of the food stores on Fressgasse lived on our street.

Another thing we who lived in Kaiserhofstrasse took pride in was the exclusive Hermannia Fencing Club at No. 11. One of its members was the world-famous Jewish woman fencer, Helene Mayer, and every time she came home to Frankfurt laden with fresh laurels, the whole street joined in giving her a festive reception. After 1933 the Hermannia moved out and the building was taken over by the National Socialist "Strength through Joy" organization. Ten years later it was the first house on our street to be flattened by bombs.

The student fraternity Rhenania also honored our street by moving into No. 19. Real duels were fought on their fencing floor. There was a Greek statue, large enough to attract universal attention, made out of sandstone in a niche at the front of the building. When no one was looking, I could pull myself up on the window ledge, and stand on the iron cellar door and get a glimpse of the students slashing and bloodying each other.

But what made our street special were the artists, painters and actors and especially singers, who lived there—the opera house wasn't far away and most of our singers were members of the company. They gave our street a free-and-easy, sometimes almost wicked character. Two rather forbidding establishments, bars that were open only at night, reinforced this atmosphere. You couldn't see what was going on inside because of the thick red plush curtains over the glass doors. For a time one of them was the city's leading homosexual hangout.

Even so, Kaiserhofstrasse was a respectable middle-class street, quite acceptable to polite society.

Nobody minded the two whores at No. 4—later on a third actually moved into our own house. They paid their rent punctually and didn't work at home. They did their streetwalking between Goethestrasse and Hauptwache, on the eminently respectable Steinweg, or around the corner on Kleine Bockenheimerstrasse, where they received their customers in a house two doors down from the Red Cat. It's the honest truth that they had their hair done every single day by Herr Jung at No. 2; they could afford it. As long as the girls—whose health was officially checked—never tried to seduce Herr Jung or his apprentices, neither he nor his very respectable wife had any objection. A customer is a customer.

My sister, Paula, was a year and a half older than me. It was she who pointed the two girls out to me and told me how to identify prostitutes: they had much thicker seams on their stockings than other women, they did it on purpose so the men would know who they were. I trusted Paula implicitly, because she was all of seven years old and everyone said she was bright. From then on I was in the know; no one could pull the wool over my eyes. You can't imagine all the whores I unmasked. They'd come tripping down Fressgasse, looking as innocent as you please, but one look at their stockings would tell me what was what. Naturally I kept my wisdom to myself.

Of course there were plenty of workers and worse on our street—because behind every front building there was a back building and there the rents were lower. You'd hear occasional complaints that there was never any sunlight in these back buildings, that they stank, and that the rents weren't all that low, considering. Take No. 10, for instance, the house next door to us. The backyard was separated from ours only by a six-foot wall with a bar for beating carpets fitted to it, which made it easy to climb over. The house was owned by a brewer's daughter, who lived on the third floor of the front building. Her husband, the locksmith August Walther, had his workshop in the yard. Their marriage contract provided that she retain ownership of her inherited property, and when talking to neighbors she never missed the opportunity to make it clear that the house belonged to her; that he owned nothing whatever but the wrought-iron sign over the outer door, consisting of two crossed golden keys, his name, and the word "Locksmith." Frau Walther shooed us away whenever we came near her house, flew into a tempest of rage if she discovered scribblings on the walls, hated all poor people because they had only themselves to blame for their poverty. If anyone complained about the rent, Frau Walther told them to move if they didn't like it, to Meisengasse for all she cared, she wasn't going to hold them back. Leaning out of her window at the back of the front house, she would shout over the courtyard so loudly that the whole neighborhood could hear them and the poor shamed complainants would close their windows and hide.

Our street was full of marvels, and I'm surprised that no one seems to have noticed them then or later. It seems to me that Kaiserhofstrasse—no one knows how it got its name*— deserved to go down in the annals of the city. Even my little scraps of memory ought to give you an idea.

At No. 6, for instance, there was a painter with the mellifluous name of Lino Salini. I've never met anyone else whose name was so well suited to his looks. What an imposing figure as he came striding down the street! Winter and summer alike he'd be wearing an enormous black hat with a brim as big as a wagon wheel and a wide flowing cape. He'd carry his artist's portfolio wedged under his left arm, while with an almost rhythmic movement of his right arm he would keep negligently tossing back the woolen muffler that persisted in slipping off his shoulders.

---

*Kaiserhof—imperial court.

Didi the transvestite, who lived in the same house, made himself less conspicuous. By day he worked in a fancy hairdressing salon on Schillerstrasse, where he was in great demand; at night he plastered himself with makeup and put on a blond wig. His favorite costumes were an ankle-length evening dress and a tight-fitting tailored suit. In either case he sported a fur stole, silk stockings, and high-heeled pumps. In these get-ups he tried to slip by unrecognized, but of course the people on Kaiserhofstrasse knew what he was up to and made jokes, which he took with a smile. I knew him well as the male Didi and his evening transformations made a big impression on me, because his gait, his gestures, and even his voice seemed to change along with his dress. If the older boys hadn't called my attention to the nocturnal Didi, I doubt if I'd have recognized him the first time.

One day long after Didi stopped daring to show himself in women's clothes, the storm troopers picked him up at his place of work and shipped him off to a concentration camp. There Didi, who'd never harmed a hair on anyone's head, except in his hairdressing, died a miserable death.

The Kummernusses lived a few doors farther on, in the same house as Mohrhard's wine bar. Two little enamel signs beside the front door, one exactly below the other, indicated their professions: he was a detective, she an astrologer, and they both practiced in their three-room apartment. Prospective clients were free to consult the sleuth in the front room or to consult the stars in the back. The prices were lower and the lamp dimmer in the back room; the quality of enlightenment was probably about the same. Obviously the two professions complemented each other.

Detective Kummernuss had rather unconventional working methods, including the theft of records, insurance fraud, bribery of officials, and in one case arson, and in the end they landed him in jail. One might have expected Frau Kummernuss to see his future in the stars and to warn him in time. But there her art failed her.

The baker's apprentice, Peter Weckesser, lived on the top floor of the same house. He was an active Communist, section treasurer, I believe, and belonged to the same party cell as Mama. He knew something about the illegal work Papa had formerly done and about our Jewish origins, but he had no suspicion of Mama's desperate efforts to cover up our past. Even after the party was suppressed, he kept bringing Mama illegal leaflets. In the summer of 1933 he was arrested and sentenced to three years in prison. I met him in the street in 1937—he had moved to a different neighborhood when he was let out—and he asked me if anything had happened to our family after his arrest, because the secret police had been watching him long before they arrested him, and several of the comrades he had visited in those weeks had also been arrested. In addition, my mother's name had been mentioned in the report of a police informer that had been read at his trial. He couldn't get over it when I told him they hadn't even searched our apartment.

I only mention this episode because it was one of our first narrow escapes.

Walter Lütgehetman lived at No. 14. His specialty was billiards, and he was world champion in his category. There's not much more to be said of him; we hardly ever saw him because he spent the whole day practicing at his billiards club on Fressgasse and was altogether the quietest, most retiring champion I ever heard of.

One of the top-floor rooms in the same house was sublet to a man named Klauer,* which was a good name for him. He got caught swiping preserves out of someone else's cellar and was sentenced to a year in jail. Neither the prosecuting attorney nor the judge mentioned the extenuating circumstances: that for the last two years he had been living on unemployment

*Klauen—to swipe.

benefits—twelve marks a week—and out of that he had regularly passed on one or two marks to his mother, though in her streetwalking days she hadn't worried about him, leaving him to the tender mercies of a reform school. Now she was living in a hospital for incurables where they didn't give her a single pfennig of pocket money.

Klauer was a genius at making radios. One day he made our family one that you could even get foreign stations on. He wouldn't take any money for it. "You're as poor as I am" was all he would say. Ten years later, during the war, we were still secretly listening to Radio Moscow and the B.B.C. on the same homemade radio.

A shiny brass plaque on the door of No. 18 indicated the office of "Corn Surgeon Joseph Walcker, consultations by appointment only." While playing "sixty-six" with young Frau Schwab's stepson in our back building, I had sometimes looked on with keen interest while she cut the corns of her corpulent, cantankerous husband. First she would soak his feet in a little tin tub, then dry them, and then, after he had personally honed his razor, she would cut the corns off his hairy toes. I could see that soaking feet and cutting corns all day long wouldn't be much fun, so I always felt rather sorry for Herr Walcker in spite of his high-sounding title.

It was this Frau Schwab, the young woman with the disagreeable older husband, who gave me my first full view of a naked woman.

Here's how it came about. The Schwabs' kitchen opened on to an air shaft, on the other side of which was a little room that they had converted into a bathroom, which had probably never yet been used by Herr Schwab. One day when I was playing cards with her stepson, Frau Schwab said she thought she'd go and take a bath. The moment she closed the door behind her, my friend dragged me into the kitchen and stationed me between the sink and the window. "Stay there and she won't see you," he whispered. He himself stood on the other side of the window. From where we were, we could look through the kitchen curtain and see clearly Frau Schwab in the lighted bathroom. She turned on the water and began to undress. I was twelve or thirteen at the time, and I could feel myself going hot and cold all over. She pulled her dress and slip over her head and fiddled for a moment with her brassiere, then with one quick tug she liberated her full breasts and cradled them in both hands, rubbing and massaging them briefly. After that she stripped off her panties, revealing a triangle of dark hair, huge and as regular as if it had been drawn with a ruler. From that day on she could wear what she pleased —trousers, skirt or coat, stripes, checks, or solid colors—whenever I met her the one thing I saw was that big black triangle.

She stood so close to the window in all her voluptuous splendor that I could see every bit of her from top to toe, every detail, each little hair, every pimple, every wrinkle. Despite the red marks her panties made on her thighs and waist and her bra straps made on her shoulders, to my eyes she was flawless, as beautiful as the Venus de Milo and as exciting as the photos outside the nightclubs. Every one of her movements made my head reel, my stomach turn over, and my knees shake. She was in no hurry to get into the tub. When she bent over to turn off the water, her big breasts swung to the rhythm of her movements. Then she spread her legs a little, stretched, showing the dark hair of her armpits, kneaded her belly and thighs and massaged her crotch with both hands. Then very slowly she stepped over the rim of the tub, turning her full-rounded behind in our direction, and gradually immersed herself in the tub up to the neck. I'd never seen a naked woman before and I almost fainted with excitement.

We peeped two or three times more; the performance was always the same, and each time I was terrified that Frau Schwab might find us out. Only years later did it occur to me that her eagerness to bathe in the middle of the day was no accident but a deliberate maneuver. Perhaps her unsatisfactory sex life had driven her to these exhibitionist games. Whatever

the reason, she provided me with an extraordinary experience.
Shrill screams were often heard from the second floor of
No. 18. The neighborhood kids said it was the corn surgeon's
customers, but I happened to know different. It was the two
lady members of the opera chorus, who lived on the same floor.
They were practicing.

I could tell many more stories about our street. About the
family of gypsies at No. 20, for instance, and how they
screamed and yelled when the storm troopers took them away
—so piteously you felt like crying with them. The parents and
all the children had to be carried down to the truck by brute
force. Or about the fat onetime opera singer at No. 17, who
never left the house without her three little dogs on a triple
leash. Or the town clerk at No. 16, who turned his whole
apartment into an aviary and cared a lot more for his exotic
birds than for his wife. One day she opened the window and
let several of his precious birds escape. And after that she
divorced him.

So you can see that Kaiserhofstrasse was a very special
street, not to be mentioned in the same breath as Meisengasse
or Kleine Hochstrasse.

The Life and Death of a Don Juan

Gustav Lapp, the saddler, lived at No. 13, across the street from us. His store fronted on the street, and his workshop was behind it. Automobiles and electric streetcars had driven the horses from the cities, and little by little the bottom had dropped out of the saddler's business.

Gustav Lapp was no ordinary saddler; he was an artist. Even among the chosen few who had made saddles to order for the cream of Frankfurt society he occupied a special place. But those days were gone forever. The only visible reminder of them was the stuffed brown racehorse, the drawing card of his shop window, not to say of the whole street. It was a magnificent Arab mare, who looked as if she were alive and wore a saddle such as I have never seen since. That saddle was Gustav Lapp's masterpiece.

The fiery mare was so striking that the leather articles displayed around her hooves went almost unnoticed, and so did the framed landscapes and still lifes in watercolor, chalk, and pencil hung on the side walls of the shop window without any relation to the other objects. For Gustav Lapp was a painter in his spare time.

It never occurred to him to abandon the trade he had taken over from his father and which had once been his whole life. He preferred to stand for hours in the doorway, looking like a statue of his past. If it hadn't been for the wall between the doorway and the shop window, you might have thought the faithful racehorse was whispering something in its master's ear.

His living quarters were on the second floor, directly above the shop. He shared them with his sister Helene, two years older than himself. Neither had ever married, and she kept house for him, as she had for many years, ever since the death of their mother when Gustav wasn't even old enough to go to school. At the time I'm talking about he was sixty-five. Helene was a nice enough woman, with a gentle, forgiving voice, but whenever I heard her speaking to her brother I could detect a note of reproach. She had been obliged to learn forgiveness over the years, because Gustav was always taking an interest in some woman or other, and that made Helene very unhappy. But, strange as it may seem, she always managed— with that gentle but persevering voice of hers—to break up his affairs and keep him with her.

Every morning Helene brushed the horse's coat, mane, and long, proudly arched tail, and rubbed the saddle and brass fittings to a high polish with a woolen cloth. But that was hardly enough to occupy her whole day, since there wasn't anybody there to create dirt. And so she would spend hours every day leaning out of the window in the parlor, where, except for her and very occasionally Gustav, no one ever set foot and which she never entered for any other purpose. Of course she could have leaned out of the bedroom window just as well, since it too looked out on the street, but she was afraid that might be misinterpreted, for it was well known that only light-minded women looked out of bedroom windows.

Placing a cushion reserved for this purpose on the windowsill, she would rest her folded arms on it. And there she'd sit. Often, as I stepped out of our house, I'd see Gustav Lapp in his slightly raised doorway and directly above him Helene at the window. I got the feeling that they were one creature with two heads joined by an invisible bar.

On Sundays it was Gustav who looked out of the window, with one difference: he never opened it. He did not sit, but stood behind the glass panes looking out. He was always alone. When he had the window, Helene never seemed to be in the room.

Gustav Lapp had his eye on Johanna Volk, who lived across the street from him, on the second floor of our house. She was the only daughter of a man who had been a butler to the last of the Rothschilds. Now and then Gustav managed to persuade his sister to invite Johanna for coffee, for a walk, or even for an outing.

One Sunday they took a long walk down the Main to Niederrad where, at Gustav's suggestion, they stopped at the Hotel Frauenhof for coffee and coffee music provided by an all-girl band. The star of the ensemble was a Spanish violinist. Everything about her was Spanish, her ancestry, her black gypsy hair with a rose in it, her musical style, her temperament; and Spanish too was every one of her nigh on two hundred pounds, which she somehow squeezed into a dress of tea-rose-colored silk with black trimmings, which had been made to encase a hundred and fifty pounds at the most.

Johanna soon noticed that Gustav had eyes only for the Spanish fiddler. The fiddler noticed it too, came over to the table and played a solo especially for the excursionists from Kaiserhofstrasse.

Half an hour later, when the concert was over and the musicians started packing their instruments away, Gustav excused himself and vanished in the direction of the toilets. The musicians also left the bandstand. When Gustav did not return, Johanna became impatient, and the two women went home on the streetcar without him.

When Gustav returned late that night, his sister reproached him bitterly. But for once he didn't take it lying down. He told her to keep her nose out of his affairs and shouted so loud you could have heard him on Fressgasse.

In those few minutes Helene's whole world collapsed. All her life she had sacrificed herself for her brother and this was her thanks. A fit of weeping brought on a severe heart attack. Gustav had to run to Bockenheimer Landstrasse and wake up Dr. Maier, who came and revived her with an injection and pills.

Helene, who had herself had such a bad deal in life, sensed the danger of losing Gustav to this late passion, for if he left, her life would have no meaning at all. But this time Gustav stood firm. He had spared his sister's feelings long enough. Every evening he went to see his lady friend, appeared in public with her, and to Helene's horror even brought her home.

Surprisingly enough, the Spanish violinist from the Frauenhof proved a devoted friend and mate to Gustav. Once she had put aside her tea-rose-colored dress—her work clothes so to speak—and removed the paper rose from her hair, the fiery Carmen became a quiet, loving, and perfectly normal woman. For Gustav's sake she remained behind when the all-girl band went on tour, and rented an apartment on nearby Hochstrasse. They would have lived together but they wanted to respect Helene's feelings.

Gustav's happiness didn't last for long, eight or ten weeks at the most. Then a terrible thing happened—terrible for those who survived it: one night in his Carmen's bed he had a heart attack and died in her arms.

Helene never recovered from the blow. She sickened, and six months later she too was dead.

And poor Carmen packed up her things, rejoined the band on their road tour, and once again squeezed herself into the tea-rose-colored silk dress with the black lace trimmings.

A Shadow on the Wall

Looking out of the window of our apartment in the back building, I faced, at a distance of some twenty feet, the gray fissured wall of the front building. Though we lived on the third floor, I had to lean way back for a glimpse of the sky. Nearby all the windows had ugly net curtains and were half concealed behind clotheslines, which seemed to be always in use. The window ledges were cluttered with bottles, jugs, empty flowerpots, and other junk. Clouds of steam rose up from the barred window of the laundry room in the basement, leaving a trail of crumbling plaster on the wall. The porcelain insulators carrying the wires that supplied the back building with electric current looked like cats' eyes in the dark. All the backyards were like that, a dreary comedown from the proud sandstone street fronts. At the center of the front building the tall, narrow stairwell windows formed a broken line culminating just below the roof in a smaller, round window. When I close my eyes, I see a shadow on that round window. Let me tell you why.

One cold morning in 1924 there was a great to-do in our front building. Cars ground to a stop outside, men ran up the stairs, women and children, bursting with curiosity, peered through half-opened apartment doors. The men climbed to the top floor and pounded on a door. A voice cried, "Open up! Police!" A moment's silence, and then again: "Open up! Police!" Doors were slammed. Somebody shouted, "Stop him!" A man ran down the stairs.

It seems he was some kind of crook or con man long wanted by the police. Only a few weeks before, he had rented a room in the top-floor apartment belonging to Herr Apfelstedt, an expert bookkeeper who, as his wife kept repeating to anyone who would listen, had never in all his life had any dealings with the police. No one had taken the slightest notice of the tenant, a man in his forties, who paid his rent punctually in advance, dressed inconspicuously, gave everyone a polite good day, and once even carried Frau Walther's heavy shopping bag up to the third floor. "The ones who look as if they wouldn't hurt a fly are sometimes the worst," said our neighbor, Frau Schmidt, the widow of a trade-union functionary, when it was all over.

Exactly what the man had done, whom he had robbed or defrauded, I have no idea, nor had anyone in the house. But who cared? What mattered was that he was a fugitive from justice and that the police had picked up his trail. But when one of the policemen grabbed him by the arm he wrenched himself free and ran down the stairs. More police, prepared for the eventuality, were waiting for him down below. Seeing that his line of flight was cut off, he ran back up again. He may have thought he could escape by way of the roof. The two policemen were waiting at the top of the stairs with readied pistols, and shouted, "Stop!" He opened the little round window, squeezed through the two iron bars, let out a bloodcurdling scream, and jumped. One of the policemen tried to catch hold of his foot, but it was too late.

Naturally we in the back house had heard the noise in the

front house, but we had no idea what was happening. I climbed on a stool and looked out. Mama was standing behind me, holding me tight; she let out a gasp, so did a lot of other people, and I saw a long shadow drop swiftly down the wall of the front building. When my eyes followed it to the yard, the man was lying on his back with arms outspread. Twice more he clapped his arms as people do to warm themselves on a cold day. And then he lay still.

It was only then that Mama noticed that I'd seen it all and dragged me away from the window. I wasn't the least bit horrified, only excited and fascinated, and I ran to our other front window to see what would happen next. More and more men kept pouring into the yard; one brought a big sheet of wrapping paper from the wine dealer's and spread it over the body. Later on some other men brought a coffin—I still remember that they were wearing black caps and gray smocks—put the body in, and carried it away. But there was still a red stain between the back entrance and the wine dealer's cellar stairs, where the man's head had come to rest. Somebody poured a pail of water over it; that took some of it away, but you could still see it plainly.

That stain where the body had landed disappeared little by little, but for days and weeks we could see it clearly. The kids at No. 12, who ordinarily played in the yard—and vaulted over the garbage carts—would form a circle around the spot and tell horror stories, one more gruesome than the next. Stories about people stabbed in the back and people stabbed in the belly; about suicides whose ghosts haunt cellars because they can never rest in peace, and when they're too tired for active haunting, they hide behind the coal piles; or about corpses that aren't really dead and wake up in their coffins. So I began to be afraid of that stain, especially after someone warned me not to step on it or I'd be sure to die this year, or next year at the latest. That taboo was observed for months, long after all trace of blood had vanished. To make sure of not stepping on it by mistake, we covered it with a handcart.

The horror story that lingered longest in my mind was dreamed up by Kurt Katscher, son of the print-shop owner in the front building. "Suppose," he said, "'that the foot of this man who squeezed through the window had got stuck in the bars so he couldn't fall. So there, with his head and arms down, he hung between heaven and earth, screaming away. So the police sent for Herr Walther, the locksmith in the house next door, and told him to saw through the window bars so the man could drop." A silly story if ever there was one, but it haunted me all the same. Sometimes at home I'd stop playing and go to the window to see if the man was hanging from the window bars. And many a time I'd actually see him dangling there with his head down when I wasn't even looking. Years later I was still dreaming about that little round window.

In the Nazi period, when we felt trapped in our apartment, expecting the Gestapo or the SA to arrest us any minute, I'd catch myself looking down into the yard to see if anyone was coming to get us. Then as I raised my eyes, they'd graze the wall and I'd see a man hanging head down from the barred round window, unable to fall or to climb back in. But it wasn't the same man any more; it was me. I'd shake my head to chase away the vision, but it wouldn't go. And even now I sometimes see myself hanging there.

The Mad Milliner

Anna Leutze occupied two large rooms on the mezzanine floor of our front building. They were on the street side and had once been offices. The disorder she maintained in them is almost inconceivable. In the one room that served as her living quarters, tables and chairs, bed, commode, bureau, and so on were buried under a dense layer of indiscriminately mingled kitchenware, clothing, and household articles. When she needed a bit of space to sit on or eat in, she would simply push aside the mess. She made her living decorating ladies' hats with artificial flowers, genuine and synthetic feathers, stuffed or imitation birds, and paillettes of every size and color. She kept her materials in dozens of shoe boxes, which filled the shelves of her workshop, as she called the second room. She worked for several millinery establishments, supplying them with spring, summer, and autumn arrangements. The floor of her workshop was always littered with hatboxes.

Anna Leutze was all skin and bones, nothing much to look at. Hard to say how old she was, maybe forty, maybe fifty. And she was a little mad, her madness being related to an exaggerated fondness for children. She made her own clothes, in which black lace and enormous cloth flowers figured prominently. She never left the house except in what must have been the biggest hat in her collection, surmounted by waving lavender plumes, and carrying a ruffle-edged parasol. She walked with short, tripping steps, accompanied by mincing movements of her torso—it made me think of a man trying to walk like a woman. If one of us boys called out to her in a special kind of singsong—"Anna Anna Leutze!"—she would put up her parasol, hold it over her shoulder with both hands, smile roguishly, and walk off more trippingly than ever.

The children of the house often gathered in the wonderful disorder of her living room. There'd always be five or six of us there, and we could do what we pleased. Our favorite game was hide and seek—we'd hide under the bed or in the wardrobe, or even in the big bureau drawers. She'd scold us gently only when we invaded her workshop—because she had her daily quota of hats to turn out and had to concentrate. Sometimes we'd playact and dress up in her clothes. She didn't mind even that. But now and then she'd ask us to make a little less noise, for fear the neighbors would complain, and then she'd bring us cookies and raspberry syrup.

She showed in other ways as well that she was wild about children. She couldn't pass by a baby carriage without bending over, burbling at the baby and complimenting the mother. If she saw a child being beaten, she would invariably step in, and vigorously tell the bully off.

That's the way she was, eccentric, friendly, and harmless. For years she lived peaceably in our midst, until one of the boys in the Kaiserhof gang discovered a way of climbing into her window by way of a ledge on the house front. After that there'd always be a few members of the gang lounging around her room or sitting on the windowsill with their legs hanging out. She had no way of stopping them and had to let them be. From then on there were no more kids playing hospital or school or hide and seek or theater in Anna Leutze's living room; it now became a headquarters for plotting street fights, especially against the Meisengasse gang.

I belonged to the Kaiserhof gang myself, though I was younger than the others and small and sickly to boot, as well as scared. I never joined in the fights, all I did was get beaten up by the kids from the Meisengasse or Hochstrasse gangs whenever they caught me. They had nothing against me personally, it was only because I belonged to the Kaiserhof gang. But beating wasn't the worst of it. One day two of the Meisengasse kids caught me, for example, and dragged me off to some backyard in Zwingergasse. There behind some old wheelbarrows, where nobody could see us, one of them twisted my arms behind me while the other calmly unbuttoned his fly, took out his pecker, and pissed on my legs. I slunk away with my trousers dripping and my tears flowing, and the two of them laughed themselves sick.

I imagine the big boys had let me into their gang only so as to have someone they could order around and make fun of. I already had sense enough to feel humiliated, but there was nothing I could do about it because you couldn't resign from the gang, you could only be expelled.

The kids in the gang—Holle, Schorschi (Georgie), Hans, Paul, and the rest of them—weren't vicious, only bored. Their parents, mostly shopkeepers with their minds full of business worries, never had time for them. Or they lived in dark back buildings with too many people and too little room and were grateful for every chance to escape from home.

Anna Leutze pleaded and screamed. She began to get angry. But it did no good, the little thugs kept coming, and as a matter of principle they always came through the window. If Anna Leutze protested too much, they'd lock her up in her workshop and scare her with ferocious threats. Things went from bad to worse, and one day they hit on the idea of making a campfire in her living room. One of them took the dripping pan out of the oven, another brought wood and paper, and they made a fire in the pan. Screaming like a madwoman, Anna Leutze burst from her workshop, picked up a broom, and flailed out at the vandals. Laughing, they dodged her blows and escaped through the window. Only one, who was not quick enough, got a few blows on the back, and sprained his ankle jumping down from the ledge. As he limped away, he shouted so loud the whole neighborhood could hear him: "Anna Leutze's lost her marbles! Anna Leutze's lost her marbles!"

The tenants, who had no suspicion of what had happened, thought she had gone mad, and notified the police. Soon two policemen from the local precinct appeared. In the meantime Anna Leutze, talking to herself in her agitation and cursing her persecutors, had put out the fire. She had no running water in her apartment and had just got back with the last pail of water from the tap on the landing. The police knocked at her door. "Nobody's coming in here!" she shouted. "Nobody!" But the police forced the door and Anna threw her pail of water at them. They decided not to press the matter and beat a retreat.

A crowd had formed outside our house. I was in the middle of it. Why I was there and not with the gang I don't remember, but I remember a good deal of what happened. I can clearly see Anna Leutze coming to her window with her hair undone and her eyes wide with horror, leaning out, shouting something unintelligible at the people in the street, then closing the window and drawing the curtains.

Nobody in the crowd, I thought, knew what had really happened. The wildest rumors were going around. According to one, the mad milliner had locked up two children in a woodshed—like the witch in Hansel and Gretel. Somebody said she was planning to kill them. Somebody else said she had already done so. Mothers began looking anxiously for their children.

"We can't just stand here while a crazy woman slaughters

our children," said one woman. "We've got to do something."
Another sent up a cry: "Save the kids! Save the kids!"

A man shook his fists. "Drag the witch out of her hole."

The crowd became restless and pressed through the doorway. A stone shattered her windowpane. In another minute the incensed crowd would have invaded Anna Leutze's apartment.

But then an ambulance from the Niederrad Hospital drove up, honking loudly, and two orderlies stepped out. The two policemen came back too, and the four men forced their way into Anna Leutze's apartment. As I was told later, they found her under the bed. The orderlies came out, got a stretcher from the ambulance, and went back in. To judge by the screams and the clatter, Anna Leutze must have put up quite a struggle. A little later they carried her through the gaping crowd. She was strapped to the stretcher and they had thrown a coat over her face.

Anna Leutze never came back and no one in our building ever heard of her again.

Expelled from the Gang

When I was ten, I had an experience that gave me sleepless nights for a long time to come. Erna, then about twelve, was the only girl in the gang. They'd admitted her because she was tough and quick and able to take care of herself in a fight. She could run as fast as the boys and was just as good at climbing walls. Her face was pale, she had blond, stringy hair. She had shot up quickly, she was skinny, with legs like matchsticks, but her breasts were already noticeable, and she was always trying to impress the boys with them. You could see them clearly— they looked like two little oranges—when she ran, because then she had a way of throwing her shoulders back and that pulled her blouse tight. More and more often two or three of the older boys would go off alone with her. One night after dark, I looked out the window and saw Erna disappear with one of them into the outhouse at the back of the yard. I got awfully excited wondering what they were doing together.

One day when the gang had met in the bushes behind the opera house—that's where we went when Anna Leutze's apartment ceased to be available—Erna suddenly said out of the blue, "Vali is a kike!" Where she'd found out I don't know, but I obeyed Mama's orders and denied it firmly. Erna stuck to her guns and said it would be easy enough to find out, all they had to do was pull my trousers down. Before I could defend myself or run away, one of the older boys pinned my arms behind my back, while another unbuttoned my fly and lifted up my shirt. I was so ashamed on account of Erna that I could have sunk into the ground. And then they all began to shout: "Vali is a kike! Vali is a kike!"

It must have been Schorschi who said there was no room for Jews in the gang, and they decided that from that moment I wasn't a member any more. They just sent me away, nobody did anything to me, Holle didn't even trip me up, which was a favorite trick of his.

This verdict was a clean and final break. I never again had anything to do with the gang. A few weeks later I was sent to secondary school and that made the separation easier. Being in secondary school made me in a way the social equal of the boys in the front building and my self-confidence, which had never amounted to much, went up a little.

When a backyard child succeeded in rising from the social basement to the somewhat higher level that a secondary school represented, there would always be class-conscious teachers, jealous of their position in the social hierarchy, to make sure that this child never forgot his lowly origins. If my work that day had not been quite satisfactory, Weyel, the mathematics teacher, would say in a kindly, fatherly tone, "Not everybody has to be a secondary school graduate. Masons and metalworkers are also needed"—a pointed reference to my father's profession. Rector Beyer, who taught us history, accused me of effrontery whenever I opened my mouth. "It seems to me, Senger—kindly stand up when I'm talking to you—it seems to me that you of all people should stop and think before talking out of turn." And one day our classroom teacher, Herr Dr. Arz, announced, "Senger and Peters"—Peters was the other "poor boy"—"have brought notes from home to the effect that they cannot afford two marks for the class excursion to the Rhine. I have a suggestion. Suppose each of you others brings ten pfennigs extra: then we shall not have to gó begging from the school board, and the two boys will be able to join us all the same. I'm sure Senger and Peters will be grateful to you."

He took his change purse out of his pocket, poked around in it with his thumb and forefinger, and held up three ten-pfennig pieces. "The first contribution," he said grandly, and deposited the coins in an empty chalk box. I'm not really sure that he added, "Poverty is no disgrace," but he might as well have. With this little gesture he succeeded not only in calling the attention of the whole class to our poverty—he might as well have written it on the blackboard—but also, with his improvised collection box, in branding us as objects of charity. I'd have preferred a thrashing.

In the years that followed, the Kaiserhof gang gradually broke up. But I saw the former members on the street almost every day. Like their parents, a good many of them became Nazis, some sooner, some later. Hans and Holle joined the Hitler Youth long before 1933, and Hans rose to be one of its top leaders; Schorschi joined the SA, and another the SS. A strip of braid extending from the breast pocket to the button-hole of her white blouse identified Erna as a squad leader in the League of German Girls. And every one of them had seen me "exposed" in the bushes behind the opera house.

We continued to live side by side on Kaiserhofstrasse. Hitler's seizure of power was followed by the boycott of the Jews, Crystal Night, persecutions of all kinds, the war. All this time I saw the boys of the gang, often in uniform, and they saw me. They even spoke to me. Each one of them could have asked, "How come you're still around? Why aren't you wearing a Jewish star? What's going on?" My heart pounded whenever I saw one of them coming. But none of them asked.

Except for Paul, whom I met one day on Fressgasse, when the war had been going on for two years. He was a soldier, home from the front for a few days' leave. He looked at me in amazement and asked, "Haven't they taken you people away?"

I answered, "As you see, I'm right here. So are my parents, so are Alex and Paula."

"No kidding? I don't get it. I thought . . ."

"You thought wrong, Paul. There's nothing wrong with us."

And Paul said, "Well, I'm glad you're not Jewish."

We made conversation for a few minutes and parted like old friends.

Around the World

There was always something going on in our backyard. People came and went, handcarts were dragged in and out, or Reiter, the master plumber, would drive his motorcycle and sidecar in with a clatter that sent clouds of sparrows into the air. I often had occasion to admire the skill of the teamsters who, with loud cries of "Whoa!" and "Gee-up!" would back their heavy wagons through the long entrance arch before executing a sharp turn into the backyard, where they would unload barrels and bottles and carry them into the wine dealer's cellar. I had no need to look out of the window to know what was being unloaded. The smell of the wine barrels was so strong that you could sniff it up on the third floor.

If you smelled cheese, then it was Petri's deliveryman transporting cheese to Fressgasse from the cheese storeroom beside the back entrance of our house, the main source of the mice and cockroaches that infested our whole building. Before taking the big cheeses away, he'd always cut them in half. This he did with a very simple tool, a steel wire with a wooden handle at one end and a loop at the other. He'd fasten the loop to a bent nail under the cart, place the wire in the exact center of the cart and the cheese on top of the wire. Then, holding the cheese down with his foot to keep it from sliding, he'd grip the wooden handle and pull the wire through the cheese.

But when the stench of burning solder drifted in through the window, I knew Wagner, the bicycle mechanic, was building a racing bicycle in his workshop. His handmade racing bicycles were famous far beyond Frankfurt.

The smell was something else again when Herr Schmidt, Janny the Persian rug dealer's driver and helper, washed carpets in the front yard, directly under our living room window. This smell suggested a mixture of old dishwater, lots of ammonia, and a dash of lilac essence. With his secret mixture, Herr Schmidt scrubbed the precious Oriental rugs so violently as to cover the yard with wisps of wool that made it look like a flower bed. At least twice after dark, long after the workshops had shut down for the night, I saw him disappear with a lady from the front building into the garage where he stored his employer's carpets.

For a while one corner of the backyard smelled of fresh paint. Something very special was going on. One of our tenants was getting ready for a trip around the world. He belonged to the great army of the unemployed. While his wife worked as a cleaning woman for five different households to fill their four daughters' bellies, he tried to make himself useful helping one of the artisans in the yard for a few cents. The rest of the time he spent tinkering and inventing. His head was always full of plans and projects, which he discussed with anyone willing to listen. He'd even explain them to me, though I was only a child of twelve. I liked him for that.

One of his ideas was a bicycle with a spring. You'd only have to wind it up, and it would go at least ten kilometers without pedaling. He had the blueprint complete in his head. Another was an absolutely reliable and foolproof burglar alarm, special for cellars, to keep people in these hard times from stealing one another's preserves, potatoes, and coal. Since he couldn't seem to get anyone to invest in his inventions, he felt injured, but he was convinced that only the hard times were to blame. His prize piece was a perpetual-motion machine. One day he took me to his room and let me look at it. It consisted of a miniature mill wheel suspended from a complicated wire frame and partly immersed in a tin basin half filled with water. When he gave the wheel a slight push, it began to turn, taking water in on one side and giving it off on the other. It really did turn for an amazing length of time. The inventor assured me that only one trifling problem remained to be solved and then the wheel would never stop turning.

One day he set up a temporary workshop at the extreme rear end of the yard, next to the little wooden outhouse that hadn't been used in a long time but still stank. There he equipped his old bicycle with a plywood structure that looked like a large doghouse and could be opened at the top and at the back. He attached an ordinary front wheel to either side of the wooden cage. A crowd of us stood watching him, and when somebody asked him what in God's name he was making now, he cheerfully explained that he had decided to bicycle around the world. Some laughed and said he was crazy, others admired his daring. In any case, he was dead serious about it. This was the great adventure he had dreamed of all his life.

For a long time he was busy with changes and improvements. On a trip around the world, he said, you had to be prepared for every contingency. For weeks he sat in his corner sawing and hammering, tightening bolts, putting the finishing touches to the interior of his rolling hut which, in addition to having a place for every possible piece of equipment a world traveler might need, had to provide him with shelter at night. It had a sliding roof adaptable to all weathers, and with the help of two flashlight batteries the inside could be lit. Last of all he weatherproofed it with several coats of oil paint. On one side he fastened a map, showing the route he was planning to take, on the other a sign in big letters: FRANKFURT (GERMANY) TO FRANKFURT IN THREE YEARS, AROUND THE WORLD.

Many a time I sat watching him while he told me why he did this and why he did that and what countries he was planning to visit. What was a year more or less when there was no work to be had in Germany? Picking up a rubber ball that was supposed to represent the earth, he showed me the antipodes —he'd drop me a line when he got there, he said. At the time I didn't know that our antipodes—if we had any—were in the middle of the Pacific Ocean.

At last the rolling hut was ready. One evening he took it out for a practice run around the block, and the next day he started. Not too early in the morning; he wanted his friends and neighbors to witness his departure. After giving his fat wife and his four daughters a parting hug, and shaking dozens of hands, he swung himself into the saddle and coasted down our sloping street. He looked around, waved his cap, rang his bell, and turned into Fressgasse, there to continue in the direction of Turkey, which was to be his first port of call.

Two weeks passed without word of our world traveler. Not so much as a postcard. His wife, if anyone asked, said it was very sensible of him to save his money, she'd hear from him soon enough, maybe he'd wait till he'd crossed the border.

And then one day, to everyone's surprise, the rolling doghouse was back in the yard. The world traveler had crept in during the night. In the afternoon he himself appeared. To the artisans and workers who gathered round him he explained with a cheerful smile that he had come back only to correct certain little flaws in the construction of his sliding roof, which had sprung a leak during a rainstorm near Karlsruhe.

He worked for at least another ten days, hammering, screwing, adjusting. Then he rode away again. This second departure was rather less spectacular than the first and three hours earlier. The announced itinerary had been slightly modified, for he had decided to steer clear of China because of the civil war. And when he rounded the corner into Fress-gasse, he only rang his bell for half a second.

The poor fellow had no luck. Four weeks later he was back, but without his rolling doghouse; he had left it by the wayside and hitchhiked. For several days he stayed home and no one could come near him. When he emerged he was a different man, not the least bit talkative. But in the end he told us what the trouble had been: boils on his seat. Three times he'd treated them and tried to make a new start, and finally he'd given up.

"I'm glad he's back," said his wife, and lovingly grasped his arm.

It remains to be told that the poor man died a year later, and his death was not at all what a world traveler would have wished. He should have been sacrificed to the gods by a medi-cineman on Papua; he and his bicycle should have stuck fast in the eternal snows of the Himalayas or the burning sands of the Sahara. Instead, he caught cold while shoveling snow—as welfare recipients had to do now and then—and died of pneu-monia.

No. 12 Kaiserhofstrasse

"Religious affiliation: Hebraic." That's what it said on our
police registration card and on the card file of inhabitants; and
that's what it said on the forged passport Papa had got himself
in Zurich. But when registering Paula and me for school,
Mama wrote under religion: "None." In the class books this
became "Nondenominational." What Mama had in mind
when she did that I never found out; she made no attempt to
tell us why we should make a secret of being Jewish, but she
was very emphatic about it, though we still belonged to the
Jewish Community at the time. We did as we were told. No
one talked back to Mama.

Actually I didn't mind in the least, because every time I
had admitted to being a Jew or been exposed as one, the
consequences had been unpleasant. And it was the same with
Paula and Alex. At grade school the class teacher, who knew
Paula was Jewish, made fun of her in front of the whole class
and delighted in telling stories about Jewish atrocities. Though
Alex never owned to being a Jew, he was beaten up several

times for taking the side of a Jewish classmate. And since he wasn't as timid as I was and didn't run away, he'd often come home in pretty bad shape.

There was something incongruous in Mama's attempts to cover up. Though most of the people in our house knew we were Jews, she kept dinning it into us children never to tell anybody. She had Alex and me circumcised with all the Jewish rites, and then she withdrew from the Jewish community. When Paula left school in 1934, Mama took her to the Employment Agency for Jewish Women on Lange Strasse, and Paula obtained work as a sales apprentice in a Jewish store. And there she stayed until the forced liquidation of all Jewish businesses in 1938.

At a time when no Aryan would dare to consult a Jewish doctor, Dr. Maier, who was known to every man, woman, and child on our street, called on Mama at least once a week for her heart trouble. She stubbornly refused to consult anyone else. As late as the fall of 1937 we were registered with the Jewish Welfare Agency on Königswarterstrasse. Every day they'd give us a package of food, free matzoth at Pesach, and in the winter coupons entitling us to buy coal at reduced prices.

A policeman by the name of Heinrich Busser and his wife lived just below us in our back building. They had no children. Frau Busser spent her days sitting on a stool, sewing and pasting soles onto slippers. When Herr Busser met me in the yard or on the stairs, he always had the same greeting: "Well, *Yiddela*, how's it going?" Then he'd pat me on the head and sometimes he'd give me a bit of change; he was very fond of children.

Another Jew in our house was Herr Strausser, a shopkeeper. We'd meet him now and then at the synagogue on Freiherr-vom-Stein Strasse. Papa would exchange a few neighborly words with him, and on Yom Kippur they'd shake hands and exchange good wishes. Still another was Max Himmelreich, a single man who worked in the butcher shop of Emil Soostmann, our landlord, and lived on the same landing as

Anna Leutze. Papa would often stop to talk to him in the yard. They understood each other perfectly because they talked the same kind of German.

*

I don't know, Mama, what was going on in your mind when you decided to erase your and Papa's origins. Were you really thinking only of Papa's revolutionary past and the danger we'd be in if it were discovered? Or did you—on purely political grounds—want to break with the Jewish tradition, with every religious and social implication of our family's Jewish roots? There were enough similar cases among your friends. Neither of these suppositions seems to hold water. I can only suppose you wanted to spare us—especially the children—the hurts and humiliations which, as you knew from your own experience, a Jew is bound to face in a non-Jewish world. Your intentions may have been good, but you could not foresee what would come of it. How could you have known that years of self-disavowal are bound to warp a man's soul and that many more years would pass before I could say without a quaver in my voice, "I am myself—the son of Moissey Rabizanovich of Nikolayev and of Olga Moisseyevna Sudakovich of Ochakov, an East European Jew, born and bred in Frankfurt, who escaped from the Nazi murderers thanks to a thousand lucky breaks."

*

It was pure chance that for a time, though Kaiserhofstrasse was not a Jewish neighborhood, there were four Jewish families living at No. 12. We were on friendly terms with all of them. There were the three Fraker sisters from Galicia, all spinsters, who lived in the front building on the same floor as the distinguished Herr Johann, the retired Rothschild butler, whose last name was Volk. The sisters were always in a good humor, though they were slowly but surely approaching an age when a woman can no longer be choosy about men. Rosalie, the smallest of the three, a tiny little thing with a bouncy, tripping gait and a round doll's face, got a husband after all: David Shimkovich, a photographer with a remarkable head for business.

There was certainly no space wasted in that four-room apartment. David Shimkovich moved in with his wife Rosalie, and a few months later they were joined by Leo, their firstborn son. The two single sisters continued to make and sell their articles of finery right there in the flat. And Leni Berger, the maid, lived there too. David used one room as a studio and another as an office. And the business did so well that he soon hired young Albert Maierhofer to do the office work. Albert didn't live in, but he, too, spent his days in the apartment.

Despite the overcrowding they all seemed happy. It was plain that married life agreed with Rosalie; her maiden sisters still sang at their work, songs of their childhood home in Poland, and in summer, when the window was open, their singing could be heard on the street. David's business flourished; marriage clearly agreed with him.

Albert, too, seemed content. In lunch hour or after work, he would play Casanova to several of the ladies in the front building. He also had a second hobby: politics. As a member of the Communist Party, he knew Mama well and our origins were no secret to him. Some time before 1933 David, his wife, and her sisters, moved out of our house—they later immigrated to England. And Albert took another job. We lost sight of him, and I didn't see him again until 1945. Immediately after the war he founded the West End section of the party and worked as hard putting up posters and distributing leaflets as he did at chasing women. The twelve dark years didn't seem to have changed him at all.

January 30, 1933

One afternoon Mama, Dr. Zely Hirschmann, and Ivan Tabacznik, a metal worker, were sitting by the window talking.
I was at the big dining table in the middle of the room, doing
my homework. Suddenly a loud voice rang out from the yard:
"Extra! Extra!" Mama opened the window and we caught the
full message: "Hitler appointed Chancellor!" And once more,
"Hitler appointed Chancellor! Extra! Extra!" Zely Hirschmann and Ivan Tabacznik jumped up and leaned out, as if they
could hear more in that position.

Mama quickly wrapped a ten-pfennig piece in a scrap of
newspaper and threw it down into the yard. The newspaper
vendor picked up the coin and put a paper on the back steps.
They sent me down to get it.

The three of them stared at the few lines of the extra.

Then Zely Hirschmann said, "I give him six months. At
the most."

Ivan Tabacznik said, "Not even."

And Mama: "A flash in the pan."

Mama Feels Guilty

One afternoon—it must have been in March or April 1933—
a commotion arose in our apartment. Some of Mama's political
friends came to see her and a conference was held behind
closed doors. At supper she announced: "Somebody's coming
to stay with us for a few days." Then, after a pause, "Somebody
that's wanted by the police. The other tenants mustn't know."

Papa shook his head in consternation. "Must we do this?
Aren't there any better hiding places? Why do we have to get
involved?"

Mama answered on a note of annoyance, "Do you think
I like it?"

I had to move out of the back bedroom with the window
on the light shaft, and late the next day our guest arrived. A
young woman, Franziska Kessel was her name. She was a Communist member of the Reichstag; I think she was the youngest
member of all at the time. She'd come to see Mama many
times and I knew her well. She had lived with Frau Röhrig, on
Adlerfluchtstrasse. When Franziska Kessel went underground,
Frau Röhrig was held by the police for two days and questioned

the whole time. She came of a good family and was unmarried, but that didn't prevent her from being a Communist sympathizer. She contributed funds to left-wing aid organizations and worked for them as well, and during the first months of the Nazi period she let the comrades use her apartment as a meeting place. When the left-wing parties were suppressed, she helped her old friends. Time and again she was called to police headquarters and questioned about people who figured on wanted lists. Twice in one week the Gestapo searched her apartment thoroughly, hoping to find information about the Communists they were looking for. Even so, I saw her later on at some of the secret meetings of Mama's little political group, which consisted almost entirely of Jewish intellectuals.

It was decided that until Franziska Kessel could find a safe hiding place she should stay with us; the comrades said it would be less risky than a hotel. Mama was terrified at the thought of a prominent Communist being found in our apartment. That's why she pressed for a brief stay. I heard scraps of an agitated conversation going on in the next room. Mama was pleading with someone to find Franziska Kessel other lodgings and move her out as soon as possible, because her connection with Mama was known to the police.

She made her point. Our guest left us the following night. A few days later she was arrested. Mama felt guilty, supposing she was partly to blame! Once Franziska had moved in, what could two or three days more or less have mattered? Her belated guilt feelings were of no use to anybody. The plain truth was that Mama's fears for her family were stronger than any ties of solidarity with a comrade in flight.

Franziska was tried in the fall of 1933 and sentenced to several years' imprisonment. Six months later she was dead. The story was that after being horribly tortured she had hanged herself in her cell in a Mainz prison.

Mama cried when she heard about it. She never said a word about it to me, but I sensed that she felt partly to blame for Franziska Kessel's death. She never really got over it.

The Toppled Monument

At about the same time as Franziska Kessel hid in our apartment there was another incident that did not directly concern our family but which, as I suspected even then, was a sign of horrible things to come. I had been visiting friends in the East End and I was walking down Pfingstweidstrasse on my way home. It was late at night and the streets were almost deserted. Then on the corner of Anlagenring and the Zeil, I saw a group of maybe ten or twelve people. That was very unusual so late at night, so I went over to see what was going on.

I stopped a few steps away from the group. They were all teen-agers. One of them turned around and scowled at me. "What are you doing here?" he snarled. "Get lost!"

I told him the truth. "I just wanted to see what was going on."

"Scram!" he snapped. "On the double!"

Surprised by his bluster, I hesitated a moment. He grabbed me viciously by the arm and threatened me: "Get going! Hear?"

That was enough for me. Besides, some of the others had noticed me by then. I beat a hasty retreat. But my curiosity was aroused; I was determined to see what they were up to. So instead of going straight ahead up the Zeil, I turned right into Seilerstrasse some hundred yards farther on, doubled back on Anlagenring, and approached the young thugs from the other direction. Confident that they couldn't see me from where they were, I crossed the street and stationed myself in an unlit doorway. It was pretty far away, but I could see them fairly well.

By then I realized that nothing had happened yet, that the action was still to come. I waited. They all seemed to be standing around an older boy, who was giving them instructions. And then they began to move; three of them left the group and went to the edge of the square, to stand guard, I later realized, against nosy passers-by. The others advanced some fifty yards to the Heine monument, which was between them and me. That brought them pretty close to me after all, and I didn't feel very happy in my hiding place.

What happened then took only a few minutes. Moving in from all sides, the young thugs attacked Georg Kolbe's two bronze figures—a young girl seated and a young man striding —with crowbars. But apparently it was not so easy; the figures were too firmly anchored to the pedestal. I could hear the sound of iron grating against stone. One of the boys climbed up on the pedestal, and while the others kept plying their crowbars, pushed the male figure with all his might. The pediment must have loosened, for a rope was passed up from below and looped around the figure. At the first heave the bronze youth fell and sank almost soundlessly into the flower bed at the foot of the monument. A few minutes later the second figure fell.

Two of the boys then set to work demolishing the bronze plaque on the front of the pedestal—a portrait of Heine in relief. That done, they all closed ranks and marched off in the direction of Berger Strasse "with calm and steady step," for they knew they had nothing to fear from' the law.

On my way home I was seized with fear, rage, and a sense of utter helplessness. Rage at what the young vandals had done, fear that this was only a beginning, and helplessness because there was nothing I could do about it.

I don't remember reading anything about the destruction of that monument in any of the Frankfurt papers. I am not sure why, because this assault on the Jewish poet Heinrich Heine must have been ordered by a higher authority and if it was to have any propaganda value it would have to be publicized as a spontaneous action of the German people against the Jewish enemy. A possible explanation is that barely two months after Hitler's seizure of power the editors of the liberal papers were so sickened by the desecration of a monument to a great German poet that they suppressed the story.

I am certain that no one but myself witnessed the toppling of Kolbe's statue. From my hiding place I could see as far as the Zeil, so I know that no one passed during that time. This action, one of the first of its kind to take place in Frankfurt, was undoubtedly carried out by members of the Hitler Youth, on orders from above. But in the spring of 1933 they were still beginners and, as it later turned out, the figures were only slightly damaged. Five years later, on Crystal Night, they had mastered their trade.

Two Dreams

For me, remembering is like pulling up water from a well. I drop a bucket, lower the rope until I feel the bucket filling with water, then slowly pull it up. The water is seldom clear enough for me to see the bottom of the bucket, and yet time and again I am amazed at all the things I find. Once I even discovered a long-forgotten dream that had kept recurring all through my childhood and adolescence.

I've been sent to Kleinböhl's store on Fressgasse for milk. As I turn the corner outside Rullmann's butcher shop, I catch sight of an unusually large animal, looking somewhat like an elephant. The face is almost human, the eyes flaming red and bulging, it's got black tortoiseshell glasses with broad bows, the kind Dr. Zely Hirschmann used to wear, and has big elephant ears that it keeps wagging. Another strange trait is that this animal is wearing a big oversized black beret, pulled far down over its head at a slant.

A beret of that kind was worn at the time by a well-known Frankfurt character, Karlchen Wassmann, and just like the elephant he wore it on a slant, pulled far down over his mop of white hair. This amiable nut rejoiced his fellow men during the twenties and early thirties by going from bar to bar clad, regardless of the season, only in a shirt, short trousers, sandals, and the famous beret, and carrying over his shoulder a green flag symbolizing hope for a better future. For ten pfennigs he sold a magazine called *Love* published by his very own self. Its contents were poems, stories, and appeals for world peace, all the product of Wassmann's pen. When he appeared in the doorway of a bar, the guests would sing in chorus: "Here comes Karlchen Wassmann, Love, Love, Love . . ." He never took umbrage at the jokes people made about him, and passed from table to table dispensing friendly greetings and hawking his paper in his characteristic singsong. *"Love* for only ten pfennigs—buy it, my dear good people, buy *Love.* " People bought it out of curiosity, pity, or just for the hell of it. After each sale, he'd say "Thank you" five times; and if someone treated him to a pretzel, the kind they used to eat with apple wine in Sachsenhausen, he'd say, "The sweet Lord repay you. I wish you a long life in peace, and please remember me to your wife."

Only an innocent out-of-towner would let Karlchen draw him into a conversation about world peace, the need to love one's neighbor, and temperance, for his missionary zeal knew no bounds.

But the Nazis objected to Karlchen Wassmann and his *Love.* Since he had no occupation apart from the publication and sale of his magazine—he referred to himself with touching pride as an "author and publisher"—they called him a parasite on the national community and sent him to a concentration camp, where he was killed.

This vicious animal wearing a beret like Karlchen Wassmann's seems to be chasing me. Strangely enough, none of the other people on the street seem to notice it, despite its enormous size and extraordinary appearance. I try to quicken my pace, but it lumbers along behind me, and the distance between us stays the same. I can't go any faster, my legs are half paralyzed; it's all I can do to put one in front of the other, it's like swimming against the current. I keep looking around anxiously, the animal seems to be taking its time, it's not getting any closer, but I can't shake it off. Somehow I know it can't move any faster, but then there's its long trunk. With that trunk it can grab me any time it wants to. And that's what I'm afraid of. I'm passing Weinschrod's fruit store, struggling desperately against the sluggishness in my legs. Some crates of oranges are piled up outside, and one of them falls to the ground. Maybe I pushed it over to block my pursuer's path. I don't remember for sure whether I intended it or not. The animal stops to pick up the oranges with its trunk and stuffs them into its mouth. This gives me a short lead. Even so, I'm still within reach of that menacing trunk. But then, at last, I reach the door of the dairy and I manage to slip in and close the door behind me.

I'm safe, because animals aren't allowed in the store. It will have to pass by. There are some women at the counter and I have to wait my turn. That's fine, it gives me more time in the store. I keep looking out through the front window, waiting for my pursuer to pass. But he doesn't appear. And then a strange thing happens. The storekeeper takes my milk pail and fills it, though it's not my turn. So now I have to leave. I open the door, which is set back in a niche, about three feet from the street.

I close the door behind me, and just then the animal in the beret comes along. Terrified, I stay in the niche between the door and the street, squeezed against the wall. Maybe the animal won't notice me. Sure enough, it's plodding past, holding its trunk out far ahead of it. I'm just beginning to congratulate myself on my escape when the animal stops right in front of my niche. I'm trapped. I can't get back because the door opens outward. Very slowly the animal turns its head, raises its trunk, and thrusts it straight at me. I let out a scream, no, it's more like a groan, and it wakes me up. I'm bathed in sweat and I can't get back to sleep.

In later versions of this dream, I realize I'm caught in the trap, that I'm dreaming, and before the animal can thrust its trunk at me, I rub my eyes and wake myself up. And it works. I wake up, I've outsmarted the animal, or at least I've escaped it one more time.

Another recurrent dream that my memory dredges up goes like this: I'm walking down a crowded street. It's always the same street, the segment of Kaiserstrasse between Frankfurter Hof and the Salzhaus, and I'm always headed in the direction of the Salzhaus. Suddenly I see that I'm stark naked.

I look to see if the people around me have noticed. Some stop, point at me, and laugh. I try to cover my penis with both hands, but it keeps peering out. Somebody pulls my hands away, I see I've got an erection! Oh, my God! The people around are laughing louder than ever.

I notice that I'm carrying my trousers over my arm. I try to put them on, but no matter how hard I try I can't get into the legs. A young fellow hands me a sack. I try to slip into it, by this time I don't care what I cover my nakedness with. But there again I fail, I keep stepping on the sack, and every time I pull it up a little way, the people pull it down again.

A crowd has formed around me; I start running. The circle opens, I pass through and run down the street with the howling mob at my heels. I look for a doorway to hide in. But the houses have no doorways, at least I can't find any, though I know there must be doorways somewhere. I run around the block several times, but it's no use. Then I see the No. 3 streetcar coming, it goes to Opernplatz, and there's a stop here. If I can get on, I'm saved. It doesn't stop; I run after it, but it gets away, my last hope is gone.

This dream, too, has variations. Sometimes the streetcar

comes while I'm in the crowd, trying to pull up the sack. But it always passes, or it's so crowded I can't get on. Sometimes a policeman turns up, and I'm scared to death because of my nakedness, and sometimes there are dogs in the crowd that bark and snap at me.

Police Sergeant Kaspar

Sometime during the summer of 1933 Police Sergeant Kaspar of the fourth district came to see us. This was nothing unusual; we'd been living on Kaiserhofstrasse for many years, and knew him well. It was customary in those days for a police sergeant to visit his "parishioners" on official business—when he needed some information or a signature or there was some form to be filled out. He usually waited outside on the landing, but this time he let Mama show him into the front room, which we'd let to the Jewish salesman, who was seldom at home. They closed the door behind them and whispered so softly I couldn't understand a thing. After Kaspar had left, Mama was terribly upset.

It wasn't until much later that I found out what he had told Mama so mysteriously. The Gestapo had instructed all the police districts to draw up lists of all persons whose religion had been entered as "Hebraic" in the police files. In this way they figured they could lay hands even on those Jews who did not belong to the Jewish Community. The police sergeant must have known that Mama and Papa had withdrawn from the Jewish community years before. Maybe she had told him.

At that time no one, not even Sergeant Kaspar, despite his concern for our welfare, suspected that those lists of Jews, which after the promulgation of the racial laws included all "half" and "quarter Jews," were being compiled in preparation for the "final solution of the Jewish question."

After telling Mama about the list, Kaspar asked her if we were planning to leave Germany in the immediate future. Mama said we were not and explained quite plausibly that it took money to emigrate.

Relatively few people emigrated in those first years of Nazi rule. Apart from those who had been active in politics, most of the early refugees were well-to-do Jews, who had money enough not only to travel but also to establish themselves abroad.

One of those able to get out in time was the butcher Emil Soostmann, our landlord. He liquidated as much of his holdings as he could and emigrated to France with his wife and their three grown children.

Six months later, the eldest son, Kurt, a young man of twenty-eight, returned secretly to Frankfurt, planning to stay only a few days. We were all amazed to see him. Why had he come? Because, in their hurry to get away, the Soostmanns had literally forgotten a safe-deposit box with valuable stocks and bonds in it. Kurt Soostmann was arrested while still at the bank. The Gestapo had discovered the safe-deposit box long since. He was shipped straight to a concentration camp without so much as a semblance of a trial, and that was the last we ever heard of him. The rest of the Soostmann family escaped to the United States after the German invasion of France.

Some days after his first visit, Police Sergeant Kaspar came back again, and again he conferred with Mama behind closed doors. He had made inquiries, he told her, and was sure that we'd have a hard time of it if our name was put on the list of Jews. Rumors were going around that the Jews would soon be moved into segregated neighborhoods and made to pay much higher taxes. And other still severer measures were thought to be in the offing. But, the sergeant went on, we needn't worry, all this didn't affect us; he'd thought it over and finally decided not to put our name on the list of Jews. When Mama asked him how he could manage that without getting himself into trouble, he explained that he had just made a little change in our registration card, he'd changed "Hebraic" to "Nonconformist." And he made it clear to Mama that she must never again put herself down as Jewish. Whenever she had to fill out an official form—and he knew that in our family it was always Mama who attended to this kind of thing—she must write "Nonconformist" or "None" in the "religion" space.

Before he left he made it clear to Mama that he too would be in trouble if it ever came out that our origins were questionable.

Why, the reader may ask, should Sergeant Kaspar have stuck his neck out for us? I honestly don't know. But the fact remains that he did. We were not close friends, we weren't friends at all. We were acquainted only through his official functions and he had never met with us out of office hours. He may have known something about my parents' political opinions, but he never wasted a word on the subject, and I doubt if he had any particular sympathy for the political organizations Mama was involved with. I saw the registration card on which he had crossed out "Hebraic" and substituted "Nonconformist" with my own eyes. The change was not too glaring because the card was full of changes reflecting changes in our family in circumstances over a period of twenty years. The change of religion was made by hand in the right margin.

But the police sergeant did not stop there. In 1935 when the so-called Nuremberg Laws—the Reich Citizenship Law and the Law for the Safeguard of German Blood and German

Honor—were promulgated and the propaganda machine was whipping up anti-Semitic feeling to fever pitch, he saw the danger of the corrected card. What if an overzealous colleague noticed the correction and started investigating our family! So he simply destroyed the old card and made out a new one. He never breathed a word about it to us. But when we had to renew our residence permit, Mama noticed the new card.

Something that happened later could have been fatal to Sergeant Kaspar, whom I remember only for his bumbling manner and his short military haircut.

It was in the late summer of 1937. Papa was standing in line at the Jewish Welfare house on Königswarterstrasse waiting for his turn to fill his big dinner pail. He had been unemployed for six years, and all that time the Jewish Relief had helped us out with small sums of money, lunches that were almost free, coal in the winter, shoes and clothing.

The place was overcrowded, all the tables in the little dining hall were occupied, and the line reached all the way from the counter to the door. Suddenly loud cries were heard, the doors were flung open, and a squad of storm troopers poured in. One of them stationed himself straddle-legged in the center aisle, and shouted, "Nobody move! Out with your papers!" The SA men passed down the rows of benches and along the waiting line, carefully examining each identification paper.

When they got to Papa, he held out his foreigner's passport. The storm trooper leafed through it, looked at Papa, leafed through it again, clapped it shut, and put it in his pocket. It would have to be checked, he said. If it was in order, my father could pick it up at the police station in the next few days. Apparently "stateless" and "foreigner" had aroused the SA man's suspicions.

The storm troopers finally left, taking with them a few Jews who had no papers.

At home Papa didn't even mention the raid, let alone tell us the storm trooper had kept his passport. He was afraid of upsetting Mama, whose heart was already in bad shape. She had told us often enough to stop going to the Jewish Relief for food; it was getting more and more dangerous to be seen there. But Papa couldn't make up his mind. He'd walk a mile to get a loaf of bread for two pfennigs less, and every evening a few minutes before the stores closed, he'd go to the food section of the Tietz store at Hauptwache, because at that hour vegetables and other perishables were sold at reduced prices. He didn't see how we could manage without those two helpings of lunch from the Jewish Relief kitchen—enough to feed a family of five.

But Mama found out soon enough what had happened. Late the following afternoon our doorbell rang. Mama opened the door. It was Police Sergeant Kaspar, and he was good and mad. I'd never seen him like that before. He stood in the doorway and asked, "Can I speak to you for a moment, Frau Senger?" Mama invited him in.

He was so furious he forgot to be careful. He spoke so loud that Papa, Paula, and I in the next room could understand every word. Were we out of our minds going to the Jewish Relief? Were we crazy or just plain stupid? Didn't we know what was going on? And then, a little more softly, if we were foolish enough to risk our own necks for a miserable dish of soup, couldn't we think of the danger to him? He'd tried to help us, he said, because he trusted us, but did we deserve to be trusted?

Ashen, Paula and I listened at the door; Papa paced the floor, wringing his hands. Then Sergeant Kaspar told my mother that a few hours before, Papa's passport had arrived at his station from Frankfurt Gestapo headquarters with instructions to examine the holder of the passport and report at once if there was anything irregular about him. He said it was pure luck the captain had been out when the courier arrived; that way the passport had come to his desk. "So what do you say to that?" Sergeant Kaspar asked. Mama had nothing to say. "Can you imagine what would have happened if the passport had fallen into someone else's hands?" Again Mama had nothing to say. "I only hope none of my colleagues noticed that I made off with the passport. Here, take it!" And out he stomped.

After that Papa stopped bringing us lunch from the Jewish Relief. He sent my brother Alex instead. That too sounds like sheer madness, and I couldn't say whose idea it was, Mama's or Papa's or both. All I know is that Papa told us that the storm troopers had only checked the grownups and paid no attention to the children, so for a few weeks Alex, then twelve, was sent for our lunch.

Still, there was nothing unusual about this seemingly incredible thoughtlessness on the part of my parents, this utter disregard of danger or blindness to it. It was fatal to Kurt Soostmann and to many other Jews. One of these was Herr Oppenheimer, the stockbroker at No. 19 Kaiserhofstrasse, who later moved to Uhlandstrasse. He thought Hitler was a great statesman and refused to leave Germany though his friends pleaded with him to go. One fine day he was shipped to an extermination camp.

*

It's a wonder, Mama, that we came through, and in part, I'm sure, it's due to your Yiddisher *kop.* * It was you alone who figured out how to pull the wool over the eyes of neighbors, teachers, doctors, and so on, not to mention the authorities. But just plain *mazel* † must have had a lot to do with it, too. All right. I can see you turning up the palms of your hands in that typically Jewish way and hear you ask: *"Mazel,* Valya? What's *mazel?"* You're right, Mama, what *is* mazel? Search me. But we did come through. And the more I rummage through my memories the more amazed I am that Papa came through, that I'm still alive and that Paula is still alive. And I wonder: Is it really possible for one family to have so many lucky breaks?

Kop—head.
†*Mazel*—luck.

"Haven't We Got Tsuris Enough Already?"

It began with trifles, for instance, those two slaps in the face I got from Dr. Runzheimer, the Nazi teacher who hardly waited for Hitler to seize power before coming to school in jackboots and the uniform of a storm trooper. He had passed out a leaflet to the class, saying that the N.S.D.A.P.* was the official government party and that we students must be loyal to the party and the Hitler regime.

Helmut Blumenstock, who was a Social Democrat, crumpled the leaflet and dropped it under his bench, but discreetly, so Runzheimer didn't notice. That wasn't enough for me. I felt I owed it to my political convictions to tear it up in sight of the whole class, go to the front of the room, and throw the scraps in the wastepaper basket.

Runzheimer let out a bellow and slapped me in the face with all his might, right, left. Then I had to go to Rector Beyer

*N.S.D.A.P., *Nationalsozialistische Deutsche Arbeiterpartei*—National Socialist German Workers' Party: the Nazis.

and report my crime. Beyer, a former officer and German Nationalist with a stand-up collar and Hindenburg haircut, bellowed almost as loud, but he didn't hit me. I was given a written reprimand and Mama was summoned to class teacher Dr. Arz. In his next class, Arz just looked at me in silence, shaking his head reproachfully, as if to say, "My boy, let's not have any more of your damn foolishness!"

But the worst was when I got home. Mama shook her fist, lamented, upbraided me. She went on and on. "You idiott!" She pronounced it with two t's in her Russian-Yiddish way. "You idiott! You'll be the death of the whole family. A piece of paper! What was the sense in it! Playing the hero, I suppose? Fighting all the Hitlers singlehanded? Haven't we got *tsuris** enough already?"

That was the last of my little demonstrations in school. From then on I contented myself with ripping up Hitler posters on billboards until I lost interest. If I'd known how dangerous that was, I'd never have done it, because I wasn't especially brave.

By myself, for instance, I'd never have dared to take on Erich Hügel, the number-one Nazi in our class, though I'm sure I'd have come out on top. His father was a house-painting contractor and an old party member. Even before 1933, Erich used to mouth Nazi slogans about Jews, Marxists, and November criminals.† He was a fanatic like his old man. If he was beaten up for his Nazi slogans, he'd only shout them louder. Even so, he was a sissy underneath, and nothing would have suited me better than to give him a good going over. But I never hit him unless Blumenstock or Kreiling, who was a big bruiser, had him in a headlock.

It must have been in May or June 1933 that I had an experience with a troop of marching storm troopers that gave

* *Tsuris*—troubles.
† Hitler called those Germans who signed the 1918 armistice terms "November criminals."

me the shudders. I was coming home from school. By the post office, not far from the railroad station, I heard loud singing. I stopped walking. A column of maybe a hundred or a hundred and fifty storm troopers, wearing caps with chin straps, was coming toward me. Pretty soon they were close enough for me to hear the words of what they were singing. "When Jewish blood spurts from the knife, Oh, won't that be the day!" That was the refrain of their marching song, so they sang it twice in succession.

I froze to the sidewalk. An image rose up in front of me: Mama and Papa and me with knives in our bellies and throats, the blood spurting from our wounds. And in the background storm troopers singing happily: "When Jewish blood spurts from the knife, Oh, won't that be the day!" And then the marchers turned off toward the station. I was to hear that song on many different occasions. And there's another SA song that has stuck in my memory. "Sharpen your long knives, sharpen your long knives, sharpen your long knives on the curbstone. Bury your long knives, bury your long knives in Jewish flesh. Blood has got to flow, blood has got to flow, And then we'll see. We say: Go fuck the freedom of the Jew democracy."

Anybody with ears could hear the songs the SA men sang, or rather bellowed—because that kind of song couldn't be sung, it could only be bellowed.

And that's why, ever since the collapse of the Thousand Year Reich, I've been suspicious of all those nice comfortable Germans who lived through the whole Hitler period but try to make people believe that they knew nothing about those things, that they'd been deceived, that all those years they hadn't so much as suspected what Hitler was really doing.

"Heil Hitler!"

For the first few months nothing much changed at school. Who cared if Dr. Runzheimer marched down the corridors in the uniform of a storm trooper and iron-studded boots as if he were on his way to the Feldherrnhalle? Who cared if his only greeting was "Heil Hitler!" Most of the other teachers still answered him with a friendly "Good morning."

Even before the Hitler salute was compulsory in the schools, he made his pupils greet him with "Heil Hitler!" He would take his stance exactly in front of the middle row of desks and "sit up on his hind legs"—that was our expression for his studied pose. Runzheimer was a very small man. Maybe that was why he took so much trouble with his Hitler salute. He laid his left hand flat on his belt buckle and at the same time raised his right arm. At the start his right hand was clenched and his arm bent at the elbow. Only at the last moment, when we all expected his elbow joint to crack because of the abruptness with which he straightened his bent arm, did the hand open and the fingers stretch just a little bit higher.

And as he roared his "Heil Hitler" into the room, he would sway slightly on the balls of his feet.

It was easy to see by the manner of greeting how quickly the Nazi bacillus infected our teaching staff. As far as I can remember, none of the teachers who put up any serious resistance. At first, it's true, most of them avoided brown shirts and riding boots. They had no desire to be identified with Runzheimer. But little by little changes were taking place.

Arz, our class teacher, was a Protestant; he went to church regularly and substituted for the "religion" teacher now and then. I imagine that before 1933 he had voted for the German People's Party or the Center Party. For a few months he went on saying "Good morning." But then one day, in response to Runzheimer's provocative "Heil Hitler," he raised his right hand just a little higher than his shoulder, opened it no wider than if he'd been releasing a bowling ball, and said "Heil Hitler." There may have been some inner resistance, but if so, he overcame it. More and more often he'd raise his arm and say "Heil Hitler," first only to Runzheimer, then to the class and everyone else. Finally, in May or June 1933, I think it was, a ruling came down prohibiting all greetings other than "Heil Hitler" in the schools. Arz's salute was always rather sloppy. He never actually stretched out his arm. He may have felt that Nazism was wrong, but as usual he adapted himself. He never expressed approval of anti-Jewish measures, but he never criticized them either, not even in the most cautious terms. His half-hearted Hitler salute could be taken to mean: You see how I'm dissociating myself from the National Socialists, and I really have nothing against the Jews, either. But what can I do?

Rector Beyer, whom we called Choker because of the choker collars he invariably wore, had yet another way of greeting. In the First World War he had risen to the rank of captain, and he wore a miniature steel helmet and Iron Cross on the lapel of his jacket. He was always in a hurry, on his way to the classroom, while teaching, while meting out punishment. He took his time only when speaking on his favorite topic, the lansquenets, the German mercenaries who terrorized a large part of Europe in the sixteenth and seventeenth centuries. He had a violent temper and it wasn't safe to contradict him. If anyone dared to offend against his conceptions of discipline and obedience, he would shout so loud that his voice cracked, and he would flail about with his stick or fists. God help anyone, friend or foe, who happened to be within reach.

Choker's greeting was always a loud, clear "Heil Hitler!" Not because he was an enthusiastic National Socialist, but because the regulations required it. He was first and foremost a German officer, and for him regulations were sacred. Still, when he saluted, the movement of his hand was as short and cursory as if he were shooing away a fly.

Of all the teachers at the West End secondary school, the only one to dissociate himself from the Nazis, though ever so cautiously, was Herr Schweighöfer, who taught us drawing. He was the last to adopt the Hitler salute. And even then his way of saluting was so comical that some of the Hitler Youth members in my class complained to Rector Beyer that Schweighöfer was insulting the Führer and the new German spirit. But he didn't change; even at official celebrations, where everybody could see him, he only raised his hand a little way, as some people do when saying "Come off it!" or "Go on!"

The Hitler spirit was most virulent in gym class. The gym teacher—his name was Otto Röhre—took the gymnasium for a training field. In his class the jumping pit became a foxhole, dumbbells were hand grenades, the horizontal bars were barbed-wire fences we had to climb over to storm the enemy trenches. Röhre was not a party member, but he was a Nazi all the same. Early in 1933, he took to wearing a little silver swastika in his buttonhole.

We spent a large part of every gym class marching around in columns of three, singing at the top of our lungs. Röhre would either march to the left of the first row or stand in the middle watching us, ready to pounce on anyone who made a false step. While the others went on marching and singing, the poor fellow would have to do twenty or thirty pushups. After every second or third pushup, Röhre would press him down to the floor. Ever since then I've felt a violent revulsion for all marching and march music. The sight of marching men—and not only in Germany—makes me feel physically ill.

Up to Hitler's seizure of power Röhre's favorite song, the one he made us march to, was "Athletes to the contest, March out to the field." But all things change, and before long we were marching to the anthem of the Hitler Youth: "Unfurl our banner in the fresh morning breeze."

My worst sufferings were in Pilo-Peter's class. Pilo-Peter was our nickname for the singing teacher, because he looked just like the little man on the "Pilo-Peter" stove and shoe polish boxes: short and fat, with a big belly and very short legs.

You wouldn't catch Pilo-Peter saying, "International Jewry is our misfortune," "All Jews are peddlers," and that kind of thing; Der Stürmer* slogans about stinking Jews and lascivious Jewish goats seldom crossed his lips. Pilo-Peter's anti-Semitism was a little subtler. He would tell "stories from real life." He had quite a repertory, and they were all about things that he had observed or experienced himself. There were quite a few about Jewish doctors abusing their female patients, raping them under anesthesia, for instance.

One of his stories was about a fine upstanding Aryan businessman whom he naturally knew well. This honest, kindly man saved a Jew from bankruptcy by underwriting a loan for him. Supposedly to show his gratitude, the Jew started coming to the businessman's house more and more often. But it wasn't really gratitude that brought him, it was lust for the man's

*Der Stürmer—the anti-Semitic newspaper published by Julius Streicher, a friend of Hitler's.

innocent thirteen-year-old daughter. And one day when he found her alone in the house, he raped her. Pilo-Peter's comment: "And that's what a Jew calls gratitude."

Here's another: A Jewish woman was in the habit of bringing young girls home from an orphanage, supposedly to give them the comforts and security of family life. In reality she was pimping for her husband who, every morning, would desecrate the flesh of these poor innocent Christian girls— since of course Jews respected girls of their own race. Pilo-Peter's comment: "What would you expect of a Jew?"

And then the story about the Jew who came to realize how vile the Jewish race and religion were, so he turned Christian. That was easy, but what about his blood? Jewishness isn't a matter of faith, reason, or feeling. The rottenness of the Jewish race is in the blood, and no Jew can get away from it. So obviously conversion couldn't make this Jew a better man, because he couldn't change his blood. It wasn't long before he fell back into his old ways and left the Christian church. Pilo-Peter's comment: "Once a Yid, always a Yid, no amount of holy water or genuflection will help."

And I had to sit there as still as a mouse, listening to the singing teacher go on about the alleged crimes of my people —all in that oily voice of his. Mama had dinned it into me that I should never express doubts, never contradict, never make myself conspicuous. And I obeyed completely: I suffered through Pilo-Peter's anti-Semitic homilies, chewed my fingernails and cuticles till my fingers bled, and kept my mouth shut.

Having to suffer in silence like that was pure misery, and it left its mark on me. To this day I apologize a dozen times a day for everything and nothing. When somebody shuts a door in my face, when somebody steps on my feet, I apologize. When I'm so glad to see someone that I hug and kiss him (or her), the next thing I do is apologize. My lack of self-assurance, my embarrassment, the self-effacement that was dinned into me as indispensable to our family's survival—all this lies behind my constant apologies.

Even when Herr Eisenhuth missed my back with his cane and made a gaping hole in my scalp, I didn't utter one word of protest, though he didn't even say he was sorry. I clenched my teeth and kept still. The wound hurt for days and I had to wear a big bandage over it. But Mama just shrugged it off and told me for God's sake not to make a fuss. Papa disagreed. "It's pretty bad," he said. "Shouldn't we maybe go to the rector?" Mama answered: "Don't bother me. You can go if you feel like it." She knew he couldn't because of his accent. And she went on, "It's not going to kill him. Haven't we got *tsuris* enough? Suppose I complain, where will it get us?" Mama stood up and paced the floor, gesticulating as if to knead every sentence into shape with her ten fingers. "He should just be careful not to get himself caned." She stopped in front of Papa, bent over him and said, "As long as Valya behaves, nobody's going to hit him." She was stirred up, because someone had dared to question her judgment, but also at the mere thought of going to see the rector. She gasped for air and dropped into a chair exhausted.

Papa put his hand on her knee and said soothingly, "Never mind. Never mind. It was only an idea." There the matter ended as far as the family was concerned. But as for me, that cut on the head still rankles.

The Family Tree

Around the middle of 1934 Herr Vollrath, our biology teacher, began teaching "racial science." One of our first assignments was to sit down with our parents and draw up our family tree. Good God! Suppose I'd come to class with the real family trees of the Rabizanoviches and Sudakoviches! Herr Vollrath would have had a stroke.

What interesting acquaintances he would have made!

One was a grain merchant from Nikolayev in the Ukraine, who used to buy the Russian peasants' grain standing, before it was even ripe, and—while his wife, Rachel, sat home wringing her hands and cursing the day she was born—spend the money as fast as it came in. That was my paternal grandfather.

Another owned a fishing fleet in Ochakov on the Black Sea and knew all there was to know about pickling fish. He pickled fish on a large scale and had plenty of money. That was my maternal grandfather.

Other leaves on this family tree would have been fishmongers, booksellers, shoemakers, tailors, coachmen, and a few members of the educated classes—teachers, engineers, a lawyer, and a doctor or two. There was even one writer. His name was Yuri Libedinski, he came from Odessa, and he was a cousin of Mama's. He wrote lots of books, a few of which were even translated into German, and he was chairman of the Soviet Writers' Union in Moscow. He died in 1959 and I never met him.

On some branch of the tree there was a *shammes* from Lochwitz. A *shammes* is the caretaker of a synagogue. And in small Jewish towns in old Russia he served as a kind of constable.

Our biology teacher might also have made the acquaintance of a man who drove around the country selling the peasants everything they needed and everything they didn't need. He was a brother of Papa's, a happy, exuberant kind of man who, like Papa, had a story for every occasion. One bitter winter's day he disappeared in a snowstorm. They thought the spring thaw would bring him back, but he was never seen again.

The paternal line boasted a few genuine rabbis. They lived and performed good works in small Jewish villages in the vicinity of Nikolayev, Kherson, and Elisavetgrad and have long been dead. But that doesn't mean a thing. Dead or alive, a rabbi is a rabbi.

If such an authentic family tree had been set before Herr Vollrath, he couldn't have failed to notice that most of my maternal ancestors were born and died in Akkerman. The Sudakoviches, my mother's family, had lived for centuries in the ghetto of Akkerman, a Russian seaport town now called Belgorod-Dnestrovski.

He might also have observed that many members of the Akkerman *mishpocheh* died on the same day. And someone would have had to explain to him, as Mama explained to me years ago, that countless members of the Sudakovich family had been killed—some beaten to death, some drowned, some burned alive—in a pogrom. The few survivors fled to the Odessa region, among them my grandparents.

For a good many members of the paternal line suffered a similar fate at the hands of the fanaticized mob and the Black Hundreds, an elite troop of the Czar's cavalry. It was a common occurrence for a detachment of the Black Hundreds to gallop through a Jewish village in southern Russia and kill a few Jews—just for the fun of it. Papa, as he once told me, had seen these precursors of the SS at work in Kherson.

And on the right and left of the page, Herr Vollrath would have found the names, written in tiny letters because there were so many to be fitted in, of all those whom famine and persecution and official decrees had dispersed to the ends of the earth.

What a wretched family tree. A monument to misery and lamentation. And I keep wondering: Why did my ancestors never defend themselves? Why in Akkerman and Kherson, why in Berdichev and Nikolayev, in Odessa and Kiev, in Warsaw and Lodz, in Frankfurt and Regensburg and so forth and so on did they lift up their hands to heaven, cry out to God, and let the frenzied mob strike them dead? And more recently millions of Jews went unresisting to the gas chambers. They knew they were going to their death, but they went. Nowhere, as far as I know, did they pick up clubs and strike out at their tormentors. Or why couldn't they have defended themselves with their bare hands? What did they have to lose?

That's how it had always been, as Mordechai Gebirtig wrote in his moving song—" 's brennt, Brider, 's brennt!" before he was shot by Hitler's soldiers in Cracow. "Un ihr shteit un kuckt azoi sich mit farleygte hend, un ihr shteit un kuckt azoi zich wie unzer shtetl brennt." ("It's burning, brothers, it's burning. And you stand looking on with folded hands, and you stand looking on while our town burns.")

There were only a few exceptions, such as the uprising in the Warsaw ghetto. There the Jews decided not to wait idly until they were starved out or shipped to the gas chambers, but to resist, to put up a fight, though they knew the fight was hopeless.

When I think of the violent death of six million Jews in crematoriums, gas chambers, and mass shootings, when I think of the dismal fate of my forebears, I can't help wondering: What kind of God is it who lets his children perish like that? Where, during those terrible times, were his prophets Elijah or Jeremiah, where were Abraham, Isaac, and Jacob? What do we need them for if they only come to life in the synagogue or in Jewish folktales, if they don't perform miracles when we need them?

But what about me? Why didn't I resist? Anyone who fought back just once or was even prepared to fight back is entitled to ask me: "What about you? You talk big, don't you? You curse God and his prophets. But what did you ever do?"

And they'd be right. I talk, I complain—when all I meant to do was say a few words about a family tree that would have bowled Herr Vollrath over.

That genealogy was never drawn up.

The one that was produced in its stead made small demands on the memory but plenty on the imagination. There wasn't a grain of truth in it, and yet it had to ring true.

So I came home and told Mama what our biology teacher wanted of us.

"Mazel tov!" said Mama.

Literally, *mazel tov* means "good luck" or "congratulations," but when Mama said it with a very special intonation, as she did on such occasions, it meant something entirely different, something like, "That's all we needed."

I told Mama what a family tree had to look like and what you had to put in it. Right away she sat down and started drawing. I could only look on. Where there was a bull to be taken by the horns, she did it. That was her way.

*

You thought for us, Mama, you learned for us, wrote for us, spoke for us, for the whole family, it was you who made all the decisions. And naturally it was you who opened the door when the bell rang and we all sat huddled in the back room, too frightened to breathe: This is it, here they come. They've come to take us away. Why, Mama, were you so afraid anyone else would make a mistake? Or was it only fear?

*

We all sat around the big dining table. Mama had pasted two sheets of drawing paper together so as to make one big sheet. Taking the names on my father's forged passport— Jakob Senger and Olga Fuhrmann—as a starting point and appending name after name, my mother constructed a purely fictitious family tree that would stand up under our biology teacher's scrutiny. Its dense foliage consisted entirely of lies. Mama let me help her and I gave my imagination free rein. Paula, who came home later, also helped us to think up racially acceptable ancestors and arrange them in a plausible order. It was no joke, because the names, birth dates, and death dates had to jibe, no matter how you looked at them—vertically, horizontally, or diagonally.

The big idea, the inspiration at the base of our work, was to situate the birthplaces of all our forebears in the region between the Don and the Volga, so as to make it look as if we were Volga Germans. This had the extra advantage of accounting for the "stateless, formerly Russian" on our passports.

Three times, five times we recopied that family tree. There was always some discrepancy, a name that didn't sound German enough, another that sounded too German. Finally, to everyone's, that is, to Mama's satisfaction, the tree was full grown and Papa gave it his blessing. Then we had another brilliant idea: we made a second copy and put it away with our family documents. It was to come in very handy—when Alex's teacher asked him about his ancestry, or when in filling out official forms we had to supply the names of grandmothers and grandfathers to show that we came of good Aryan stock, and so on. With our copy there were no problems, we could be sure of getting our ancestors' names and dates straight. As it happened the family tree—which had seemed such a nuisance at first—was to provide our house of lies with a sturdy prop.

Still, our family tree had one weakness that couldn't be helped and that might have proved fatal. If my parents were Volga Germans, how come they were born in Lithuania? When having his passport forged in Zurich, my father, we never knew exactly why, had given Vilna as his and his wife's birthplace, and so it appeared on all the official registers. Maybe his idea had been to cite a birthplace as far removed as possible from his real birthplace in the Ukraine, because in the Ukraine he still figured on all the wanted lists. But it's equally possible that his pronunciation was to blame and that he'd meant to say something entirely different. What makes this theory seem plausible is that the name of *Senger,* as my father once owned to me, was due to a mistake in spelling.

This is what happened. When the forger asked him to choose the name he wanted and write it on a sheet of paper, he wrote *Jakob Senger* with an *e.* It should really have been *Sänger* with an umlaut. For a Russian Jew, wanting to give himself a false but nice-sounding German name, Sänger (Singer) was a good choice; it made him think of the *hazan,* the cantor, at the synagogue; a pleasant image to carry around with him. Unfortunately my father had never heard of the German letter *ä,* which is unknown both in Russian and Yiddish. So he wrote Senger with an *e,* and that is how I spell it to this day.

A trifling mistake, you may say. But many years later it was to have momentous consequences—thanks to Rector Beyer, the man we called Choker.

Choker's hobby, as I've said, was the history of the lansquenets. One day in class he strode along my row of benches and stopped in front of me. "Senger, stand up."

I jumped up. What did he want? What was wrong?

"Senger, have you ever stopped to wonder who you are, whom you are descended from?"

How could this have happened? How could Choker of all people have fathomed our secret? Or had he? Was this the moment of truth? I stammered, "I d-don't know."

"But you should know. Don't you agree?"

"Oh, yes, sir, of course."

"Well, then I will tell you. You are descended from Mad Christian."

Whew! What a relief! I hadn't the faintest idea who Mad Christian was. But I did know that as an ancestor he was a thousand times preferable to Moissey Rabizanovich of Niko-layev.

"From Mad Christian," he repeated with emphasis. "Mad Christian was the notorious Duke Christian of Bruns-wick, the most dreaded of all the lansquenets in the Thirty Years War. Wherever he and his savage band appeared, they pillaged and killed and set the peasants' huts on fire. One of your ancestors must have belonged to Mad Christian's band and distinguished himself in pillaging towns and villages. After pillaging a town, he undoubtedly set fire to it, and that's how he came to be nicknamed 'der Senger'—the scorcher. You understand?" I nodded. "You see, every family name has its history, and some of these histories are very interesting."

From that day on until I left school, the rector called me Mad Christian, and so did my classmates. And all because Papa was unacquainted with the German letter ä.

My father's bad German was to blame for another mis-understanding. In 1917, when my sister, Paula, was born, he went to the town clerk's office to have the birth registered. The family, Mama, that is, had decided to call her Paula Esther. Paula because it was a good German name and Esther in honor of the Jewish queen who had saved the Persian Jews. My father had no trouble with Esther—as a child during Purim festivities he had vigorously swung the *grager*, the wooden rattle, to drown out the name of the villain Haman whenever it was spoken. This Haman had wanted to kill all the Jews, but he had been foiled by the wily Esther. So my father had no trouble with Esther. But that diphthong *au* in Paula was tricky. Papa had been warned. He'd made a fool of himself with Senger, and he shouldn't let it happen again. He scratched his head. He knew it took more than one vowel to produce the sound *pau* But which ones? Very neatly he wrote *Pau*. But then he hesitated. Two vowels? Only two? The Germans were such sticklers, one couldn't be too careful. Suddenly the vowel *o* flashed up in his mind. Now that's an attractive vowel. To pronounce it, you have to purse your lips as in singing. What harm could there be in throwing it in? Too much is always better than too little. And so Papa, in his sharp, angular script, gave his newborn daughter the name of *Pauola*. And more than half a century later the name in my sister's passport reads: *Pauola Esther Senger*.

Of our many lucky breaks this was perhaps the strangest. In all the official documents my sister's middle name was entered as Esther, as typically Jewish a name as Sarah, Golda, or Rachel. But in all the twelve years of the Thousand Year Reich no one asked any questions about it, no one raised any objection, or pointed at my sister, saying, "That girl must be Jewish." Every time we had to fill out an official form, to renew our residence permit or Paula's working papers, that middle name almost drove us to despair. Mama groaned, Papa wrung his hands, and one of them regularly said, "We can only hope for the best."

Our biology teacher looked with amazement at the Senger family tree—all these people on both sides, living between the Don and the Volga, in the region where the Volga Germans dwell, with the obvious exception of our immediate family, who had somehow come to Frankfurt.

Why, he asked me, had my parents left the peace, the shelter, the security of their Volga-German homeland to settle in Frankfurt? Mama hadn't prepared me for that one, so I couldn't think of an answer. But it didn't matter. Our family tree impressed him and he studied it carefully.

A few weeks later when discussing the various Aryan races, he called up a few of the pupils and took their skull measurements. For this he used a strange instrument, which looked like a big compass bent at the end. And he'd brought some charts and tables with him.

I was the first to be called. He was determined to show his astuteness as a racial analyst. Applying the arms of his crooked compass to my head, front and back, left and right, he wrote down figures. The class watched him attentively. He took one chart, then another from his desk, held them up to his thick eyeglasses, wrote figures on the blackboard, added, subtracted, multiplied. When he had finished, he turned to the class and announced triumphantly: "Senger—Dinaric type with Eastern admixture. Aryan race, sound to the core." Herr Vollrath was pleased with himself and with the result of his first skull measurement. No wonder. He had studied Mama's family tree with care.

The Suitcase

Why none of the many pitfalls along my path proved fatal to me, I shall never know, nor can I explain why none of the traps closed on me. I can't count the number of times I sighed with relief and said to myself, "Well, it looks like I made it again." Trembling, I'd go on with my tightrope walking, sure that the next little slip would seal my doom and that of the whole family. So it was easy for Mama to hold us in check. She didn't have to raise her voice. Every word she said had the ring of authority. Nobody ever thought of answering back.

Mama brought us up and Papa helped with the little things, like playing parchisi with us or taking us for walks. It was Mama who made all the important decisions, such as when to go to school and when to leave it. When she decided that a secondary school certificate was enough for Paula, Alex, and me, Papa agreed with her as a matter of course and helped us with our homework. Many's the time he said to one of us, "What more do you want? Didn't you hear what Mama said?" Or: "*Oy vay,* if Mama finds out!" He loved her with all his heart. I never heard him say a harsh word to her or about her. Toward the end the precariousness of our existence got to be too much for her heart. Her pulse became more and more irregular, and the doctor couldn't help. My father took care of her for months and years, to her dying breath.

Up to 1937 Mama and her group had no trouble keeping contact with the comrades who had emigrated to France. After that it seemed to be harder. Once when it was necessary to send some papers to France, and set a date, Mama decided that I should be the courier. I suppose no one else was available at the time. She told me it was perfectly safe because my name didn't figure on any list of political suspects, and surely, with the thousands of people who crossed the border every day, no one would notice me.

In 1937 it was still easy enough to leave the country, even with a foreigner's passport. Mama's niece, Taya Baumstein, was living in Toulouse. She asked Taya to send me a formal invitation. When it came, I took it to police headquarters and they gave me an exit visa right off. Then I went to the French consulate, and there was no trouble about a French visa either.

Two weeks later I was ready to leave. There was an international fair going on in Paris at the time. Lots of Germans were attending and we were sure nobody would notice me in the crowd. I'd just have to board an express train at Frankfurt Central Station and get off at the Gare de l'Est in Paris. No need to worry about being checked on the train, because my passport was in order, visas and all. My trip even had a plausible purpose: visiting a relative who actually existed.

It was all very simple. The small package and a few letters, which I had carefully hidden, did not make the trip any riskier. I remember there was a letter for Dr. Zely Hirschmann and a letter or two from Eva Steinschneider, who was still living in Frankfurt, to her husband, formerly a well-known defense attorney, who had had to leave Germany not only because he was a Jew but because he had defended left-wingers in court before 1933.

But then the business with the suitcase came up. Two days before my departure, Mama and her friends decided I should take a suitcase to Paris. They thought the opportunity was too good to miss. The suitcase belonged to Liesel Ost, a bookseller who had lived in our neighborhood, on Hochstrasse, with a Rumanian Jew. The Gestapo had been watching her because of her connection with an illegal group. At the end of 1935 she decided to go to France with her lover. They had left in a hurry and taken only strict necessities. She had put her jewelry, a few personal articles, and a savings bankbook, covering a considerable sum that she hadn't been able to withdraw from the savings bank in time, in a small suitcase, which she left with a comrade who lived on Kleine Hochstrasse and who offered to keep it until there was an opportunity to send it to her.

Liesel Ost and her friend had spent the night before leaving with us, because their apartment had been searched and they were afraid of being arrested at the last moment. That night Liesel Ost told Mama that whoever called for the suitcase at the Kleine Hochstrasse address should identify himself by saying, "I've come from Augsburg."

Having to cross the border with that suitcase was bad enough, I thought. And now Mama was sending me to Kleine Hochstrasse to pick it up.

I hadn't far to go. Kleine Hochstrasse is a short street. No. 8 was almost directly across from where the Club Voltaire is now.

It was dark on the steep stairway and the rickety steps creaked every time I put my foot down. The comrade who'd been given the suitcase for safekeeping lived on the top floor. Mama knew him but had lost touch with him since 1933. There was no landing at the top, the staircase ended at the apartment door, so I had to stop on the next to last step. I took a deep breath and turned the bell knob. The sound was like a bicycle bell. No one opened. I rang again, louder and longer. Then there were steps and the apartment door opened, but only wide enough to pull the security chain tight. Above me, in the space between the door and jamb, a woman's head appeared.

"Good afternoon," I said. "Is your husband home?"

"What do you want of him?"

"I've got to see him."

"My husband is sick."

"It's urgent."

"Couldn't you come back another time?"

"I'm afraid not. But I won't stay long."

"Wait."

The door closed; I stood on the stairs and waited. It seemed like a long time. I was beginning to sweat. Finally the door opened, but the chain was not removed. A man peered out. He was wearing a sleazy blue bathrobe. I was pretty sure I'd seen him before.

"What is it?" he asked.

"I've come from Augsburg."

"So what? Who cares where you've come from?"

"Liesel Ost sent me."

In that moment a change came over him. I could see the man was terrified. "Liesel Ost?" he said. "Liesel Ost sent you? What does she want?"

I said it again. "I've come from Augsburg. Liesel Ost sent me . . ." And after a short pause I added, "You can trust me."

"What's that supposed to mean?"

"I've come for the suitcase."

"What suitcase? I don't have any suitcase."

"Liesel Ost's suitcase."

"I don't have any suitcase."

"But you must have it."

"I must, must I? Who are you anyway?" By then he was

shouting. With a trembling hand he removed the chain and flung the door open. Standing barefoot on the step above me, he shouted so loud the whole stairwell echoed. "Who the hell are you? That's what I want to know."

"A friend of Liesel Ost," I whispered, "and I've come for the suitcase she left with you."

He shouted at the top of his lungs. "Can't you hear? I don't have a suitcase. You trying to make a fool of me?"

I heard doors opening on every floor. A man's voice shouted, "What's going on up there?"

He leaned down over the banister and said, "Never mind. I can handle this." And turning to me—"All right. How about it? Do you still want a suitcase?" And thrusting his face close to mine—"Beat it now, if you know what's good for you."

I was too scared to move. He grabbed me by the shoulders and shook me. "What's the matter? Are you stupid? I'm not having any truck with Communists, understand? So beat it or I'll call the police!"

I understood him all right. I went down the stairs in a daze. At every floor people came out and stared at me. Nobody said anything. Nobody stopped me. I felt so weak I had to keep hold of the banister. When I was almost at the bottom, somebody called after me: "Damn Communist swine!" Some kids were playing in the entrance. I ran past them and out into the street.

When I told Mama what had happened on Kleine Hochstrasse, she clapped her hands over her head. "I'd never have expected that of him!"

I had to repeat the whole story from start to finish. "Do you know if he recognized you?"

"I don't know. He didn't say anything."

"Did he ask you your name?"

"No."

"Or who sent you?"

"No, he didn't ask me anything."

Then Mama let go with the worst insults she could think of: "The *chozzer!** He should burn! He should drop dead!"

Two days later, I took the train to Paris with the letters and the parcel but no suitcase. The trip was uneventful. No trouble at all.

Liesel Ost's suitcase never turned up. During the German occupation, she was active in the French Resistance as a courier. She died a terrible death in 1944, after the SS captured her. They thought she could give them information about the French Resistance, so they tortured her. She didn't tell them a thing and she died under the torture. Her mutilated body was found in an abandoned farmhouse near Lyons. She had been blinded before she died.

My memory is full of seemingly unrelated fragments, which in retrospect connect up with the important events of the time.

For instance, there was a woman to whom Mama often gave small sums of money, three marks, four marks, sometimes as much as ten; Mama was scared stiff whenever she came around. Mama never said a word about her to me, but from dibs and dabs that I overheard I figured out that this woman knew we were Jewish.

Then my mind registers a picture of a man being hauled out of his house by the police just as Papa and I were on our way in to see him. Who he was and how he was connected with our family, I don't remember. Nor can I imagine why Papa and I weren't even stopped.

I remember a Hanukkah celebration of the Jewish congregation on Baumweg, which I attended. Suddenly a gang of Hitler Youth burst into the hall, formed a ring around us, and chanted: "Jews, get out!" and "Go home to Palestine!" That was the end of the ceremony. We all had to leave.

And another incident flashes through my mind. Though

*Chozzer—pig.

it placed our family in great danger, I can't fit it into any context. One cold December day—it may have been in 1937 or 1938—a man came to our apartment. He showed us his discharge from Butzbach prison, and asked us to put him up for a few days. He said he was on his way to Nuremberg, but first had some business to attend to in Frankfurt. As reference he gave the name of a Communist well known to us, who was still doing time in Butzbach. Mama didn't like it, but she couldn't very well send him away. I still remember his nickname, Moro. On the second or third day he went out and never came back. A week later we heard by accident that he'd been arrested in Bornheim with some other comrades. We were worried sick. We thought he'd tell the Gestapo where he'd been staying in Frankfurt. He'd left a suitcase with nothing in it but toilet articles and soiled clothes. We took it down to the cellar. The days passed. The Gestapo didn't come. Moro hadn't spoken.

Rivalries

There were two competing plumbers on Kaiserhofstrasse: Konrad Bämpfer at No. 7 and in our house the red-headed Otto Reiter. Konrad Bämpfer rode a bicycle to his jobs and took to wearing a brown uniform long before 1933. His competitor, Otto Reiter, was a motorcycle enthusiast, the proud owner of a Horex, and no Nazi.

Otto Reiter was also an inventor. One of his inventions, a device for sprinkling shop windows, was a big success, and soon he had orders from all the florists for miles around. After that he was too busy to bother with the usual little repair jobs like fixing leaky faucets, unplugging toilets, and so on, and he'd turn them over to his competitor. In addition, he could now afford to equip his shop with various machines that were to come in very handy during the war.

He spent most of his spare time tinkering with his motorcycle, an enormous thing with a sidecar. Aside from that, his main weakness was red-headed women—as red-headed as himself. I knew three of his girl friends. One was the skinny salesgirl at Emmerich's butcher shop. When I asked for a quarter of a pound of liverwurst, she was so afraid of giving me too much that she almost cut her finger slicing it. At closing he'd be waiting with his motorcycle on Kleine Bockenheimer-strasse, outside the back door of the shop. The second looked anemic and was married to a barrelmaker. The story was that the husband came home unexpectedly one day and caught them *in flagrante*. The third was Käthe; she was about thirty with the luscious sort of build that is best described with both hands. I have a pleasant memory of her. But the story requires an introduction.

One day in the spring of 1939 Otto Reiter saw me in the courtyard and called me into his workshop. He closed the heavy door behind him and told me that Konrad Bämpfer, who usually avoided him, had dropped in to make inquiries about our family. He'd been sent by the local party group, in which he took a leading part. Bämpfer had asked him what he knew about us; was there any truth in the rumor that we were Jews? Could Reiter question the other tenants about us? He had assured Bämpfer that we couldn't possibly be Jews, that everyone in the house would know it if we were, that we certainly didn't act or look like Jews, that the basis of the rumor could only be some malicious denunciation, that he personally had only the best to say of us, we were good neighbors and national comrades. After telling me all this in a tone from which I could gather that he knew better, Otto Reiter added that it was none of his business who we were or where we came from, he never listened to gossip, but I and my parents had better beware of Bämpfer. I was shaking like a leaf when I left his shop.

At about the same time Frau Walther on the third floor asked Frau Volk on the second floor why our family was left alone when so many Jews had been relocated. Not only were we Jews, she said, but foreigners as well, and Herr Senger couldn't even speak German properly. Frau Volk knew perfectly well that we were Jews. But she played innocent and said it wasn't right to spread such dangerous rumors about us in times like that. She assured her that Frau Senger had showed her police certificates proving we were Aryans, authorized to stay in Germany indefinitely.

Three years later, in the war year 1942, an entirely different incident reminded me of my conversation with Reiter and his warning against Bämpfer, and it was no less dangerous this time. Käthe Fröhlich was a florist's helper. Otto Reiter had met her in a florist's shop where he was installing one of his sprinkler systems. At that time, thanks to the machines he had acquired, he had expanded his shop and was making some sort of "war-essential" fittings for the government. This war work made it possible for him to have Käthe requisitioned and transferred to his shop.

One time when I dropped in, she seemed extra friendly, so I got into the habit of going there pretty often. I could see Reiter didn't like it; he was very jealous. So I'd pick times when he was out on his Horex. Käthe wore tight-fitting overalls at work; I'd chat with her and help her a little. She'd brush against me when she could; that encouraged me, I'd put my arm around her waist and give her a squeeze, she'd laugh and snuggle up to me. We never went any further, because there was no way of knowing when Otto Reiter might turn up. We couldn't hear his motorcycle, because Kaiserhofstrasse was on a slant; he'd switch off the engine at the far end and coast right into the court. So you were never safe from him.

After a while I found out that Käthe flirted and cuddled with every man who came to the shop. But that didn't keep me away. Otto Reiter was bound to catch us sooner or later. When he did, he spoke very slowly, in a voice that sounded calm—on the surface. "Don't push me too far," he said. "Have you forgotten about Bämpfer and the interest he took in your family?"

Luckily Käthchen, who was standing right near us, didn't ask for an explanation. I left the shop in a hurry and never set foot in it again as long as Käthe Fröhlich was working there. There was a deadly threat in Otto Reiter's words, but he was certainly not an informer. I'm sure he knew all about us, and he could easily have reported us to the party or the Gestapo. It doesn't take long to tell the rest of the story. The house where Käthe lived was destroyed by a bomb. Thanks again to his war-essential work, Otto was able to have her moved to an apartment at No. 19. The previous tenant had just been taken away by the Gestapo. Reiter even left his family and moved in with Käthe for a while. But the romance didn't last long. Käthe got herself a lover who was twenty years younger than Otto and had black hair. The plumber returned to No. 12 Kaiserhofstrasse. Käthe gave up her job in his workshop and went back to the florist's with Otto's sprinkler system. After that he had more time for his Horex.

Max Himmelreich

The few Jews who still lived in our street after Crystal Night were taken away to concentration and extermination camps in the first years of the war. There were the musician and his wife at No. 7, Herr and Frau Bach at No. 14, and a traveling salesman in the same house. The Grünebaums at No. 16 were said to have committed suicide after their nineteen-year-old son was taken away.

Max Himmelreich, an old man who had been working for Soostmann, the butcher, was sent to Dachau. To everybody's amazement he came back five months later, shorn bald and even more stooped than before. Why they had let him go I don't know, neither did he. He moved back to the little room on the mezzanine floor of the front building; he'd always been inconspicuous, and now he was even more so. He left the house in the gray of dawn and took the train to Bad Soden in the Taunus Mountains, where he worked in a brick factory along with other conscripted Jews. He came home late in the evening and crept into his room. Before his stint at the concentration camp he had often talked with me and the other tenants, especially with Papa. Now he hardly spoke to anyone. Several times I saw him deliberately avoiding people in the house and on the streets.

One evening, when he came home from work, I almost bumped into him on the stairs. He begged my pardon and flattened himself against the wall; then he said in a tone of relief, "Oh, it's you, Vali." He'd always had the peculiar habit, when talking to me, of putting my name into almost every sentence. He tried to slip by, but I deliberately blocked his way.

"What's the matter, Max? You never speak to me any more."

"Don't ask me, Vali," he mumbled. "I'm not allowed to. Let me go."

"Did they tell you that at the camp?"

"Yes, at the camp." He looked furtively behind him to make sure no one was listening. Then, thrusting his face close to mine, he whispered in his hoarse voice, "They beat me, Vali."

"Bad?"

"Very bad!"

He clutched his head in his hands as though to stress the horror of that event. Then after a while he climbed the few steps, pulled his key out of his pocket, and opened his door. Motioning me to come into the doorway where no one could see us, he said in an undertone, "Watch out for those people, Vali." He pointed at the apartment where Anna Leutze, the mad milliner had lived. Then he went into his room and closed the door behind him.

Since Anna's days the Feist family had moved in. He was an invalid, she worked as a cleaning woman. Everyone in the house thought that they were Gestapo informers, that they reported everything that struck them as suspicious and had been responsible for sending Max to Dachau. When to our surprise he came back, Frau Feist made it clear to all who would listen that she, a good German woman, had no intention of cleaning outside the door of a dirty Jew. She was as good as her word. The little patch of landing outside Max's door was never swept and never scrubbed.

I was fond of Max. He was a good-natured, helpful soul. The day they dragged Anna Leutze out from under the bed and took her away to the asylum, he actually wept. And he was always good to us children. One time he helped me out of a bad fix.

Outside our house there was a gas lamp on a cast-iron post. About three feet from the ground this lamppost had a little ledge where you could rest the edge of your foot. Higher up there was a small crossbar for the lamp cleaner to lean his ladder on. The big boys in the gang could stand on the ledge, shinny up the pole, and do gymnastics on the crossbar. When they'd had enough, they'd wrap their legs around the lamppost and slide down.

One day Schorschi came up to me, looking as if butter wouldn't melt in his mouth, and asked me, "Want me to help you up?"

"Sure," I said.

"All right. Let's go." He climbed on the ledge, grabbed me by the arms, and lifted me until I could grab the crossbar with one hand. "Hold tight!" he said, then he let me go and slid down the pole. "Hold tight now!" he said again, and disappeared.

I was scared to death. I yelled for all I was worth. I was able to wrap my legs around the lamppost like the big kids, but I was afraid to let go of the crossbar. At that point Max Himmelreich, with nothing on but his trousers and bedroom slippers, came running out of the house and plucked me off the lamppost like a ripe apple.

One day Max stopped me in the dark entrance to our house and spoke to me—something he hadn't done for months.

"Could you come to my room for a second, Vali?" Without waiting for an answer, he padded up the stairs, opened the door, and went in. I followed him. He closed the door but didn't turn the light on. "You knew I had to wear a star?" he said, and showed me the yellow star on his jacket. An order had recently gone out that all Jews had to wear them.

"Aren't you people Jews?" he asked.

"You know we are. Why do you ask?"

"Don't get me wrong, Vali!" Max was embarrassed. "I only wanted to say that I'm worried about you."

"Aren't you worried about yourself?" I asked.

He shrugged. "Who am I, Vali? An old man, no good for anything." Max couldn't have been over fifty. He went on, "But you and Paula and Alex, you're still young." And still standing in the dark, Max told me how he had heard from the other Jews at the brickworks in Bad Soden that the stories about Jews being resettled in the East weren't true. They weren't being resettled at all. No, they were being shipped to camps where they were killed. He grabbed me by the arm for emphasis and implored me: "Get out of Germany if you possibly can. You and your family. Get out quick." He said we were in great danger, he knew it for a fact. "That's all, Vali," he said. "You can go now."

A year later the SA took him away a second time. It was early in the morning and nobody in the house noticed. We didn't find out till a few days later, when the police opened his door and his wretched bit of furniture was hauled away.

Max Himmelreich never came back again.

Crystal Night

In 1935 I started my apprenticeship as a mechanical drafts-
man. Mama wanted me to. I don't much like to think about
those times, not so much because I was fired in the third year
of my apprenticeship but because I can't help remembering
two very disagreeable fellow workers. One was an asthmatic
chain-smoker. He had chronic catarrh and kept hawking and
spitting into his handkerchief. After every cigarette he'd spray
his throat with the help of a squeaky rubber bulb, so our
drafting room stank of camphor and eucalyptus from morning
to night. The other was a homosexual SS man. He'd come up
behind me as I stood at my drawing board, pretend to have
something important to explain to me, and press his swollen
sex organ against my thigh. He did the same with the other two
apprentices. He'd take care not to follow me when I took a
quick step sideways. Though I've never been attracted to
males, the contact excited me, because up until then Mama
had managed to keep me away from girls. That made me more
vulnerable to homosexual propositions than other boys of my
age. It was more dangerous when the SS man followed me to

the toilet. While we were shaking off the last drops, he would suggest we inspect each other's cocks. The two other apprentices consented, and I might have, too, coward that I was, if I hadn't been afraid he'd notice I was circumcised.

One day during lunch hour one of the apprentices pinned a drawing on the SS man's board; it showed a death's head, but this death's head wasn't the symbol of the SS; it was more like the skull you see on poison bottles, except that the crossbones were two erect penises.

That drawing put a scare into him and after that he spared us his attentions. Still, he was lucky; no one ever reported him. I ran into him once during the war. He'd been decorated several times for bravery.

A crippled stockroom man was responsible for getting me fired a year before the end of my apprenticeship. We apprentices used to play tricks on him, and once when he had a chance to get even, he pounced. He caught me in the Italian ice cream parlor on Frankenallee during working hours and not only reported my offense to the manager, but added that I'd stolen some pencils, which was a malicious lie.

My dismissal set off a storm in the family, mostly because it attracted attention, and that was the worst thing that could happen to people who were trying so hard to make themselves invisible. Mama was called in to see my boss, who told her why he was rescinding my apprenticeship contract. The evening of that day was loud with reproaches, screams, and tears, and ended with Mama having a heart attack and Papa flailing his arms in despair.

When we had all recovered from our exhaustion, and from my shame, someone thought of Mama's old friend Fanny Ritter, who was Jewish like ourselves and on familiar terms with Remy Eyssen, president of Fries Jr., the well-known steel construction firm. If she could persuade him to let me finish out my term of apprenticeship with his company, I'd be saved.

Fanny Ritter didn't hesitate for one moment. She told Remy Eyssen who I was and what had happened, but threw in the pious lie that on completion of my apprenticeship I planned to go to Palestine.

The miracle came to pass, he hired me, a Jew—in the year 1938. I wasn't assigned to the main plant in Riederwald, but to the smaller one in Sachsenhausen. Before I started work, Remy Eyssen called me into his office and told me he wasn't interested in my story, just so long as I behaved myself and left the firm on completion of my apprenticeship. I promised both. And I really did my level best to keep out of sight—until November 1938. Then came Crystal Night.

"Oy vay, what will be now!" cried Mama, when the news came over the radio that a certain Herschel Grynszpan had shot Ernst vom Rath, secretary of the German legation in Paris. The murdered man came of an old Frankfurt family. Mama held her head in her hands and her eyes were big with terror. "It's all they were waiting for," she gasped. And then, dwelling on every word, "What the Hitlers have done to us so far is nothing compared to what's coming now."

As usual Mama was right. Next morning as I was crossing the iron footbridge on my way to Sachsenhausen, one of the typists overtook me. "Heard the news? The synagogue on Börneplatz is on fire. They're smashing the windows of all the Jewish stores on Sandweg and throwing everything out in the street."

The office was in an uproar, all talking at once, everybody with something different to report. The new synagogue on Börneplatz wasn't the only one, all the synagogues were on fire. All over the East End and North End, Jews were being driven from their homes, all the Jewish shops were being smashed up.

I waited for the Hitler Youth member who worked at the drafting table in front of me in "Construction." He was two years older than I and in his last year of apprenticeship. He often came to work in his Hitler Youth uniform, with a strip of braid looped from one shoulder strap to his middle shirt button, his insignia of rank as a squad leader. He was always the first to know when some new action was to be taken against the Jewish population.

I was awfully stirred up, but I had to be careful not to arouse suspicion, not to show more curiosity than the others. Finally, I couldn't stand it any more, I put on my coat and ran to Börneplatz. When I was still far away, I saw a big cloud of smoke in the sky.

Then I stood in the crowd on the square, watching the flames rise from the big dome. About a hundred yards from the burning building, the SA and auxiliary police formed a cordon to keep the crowd from getting any closer. Up ahead of me, just beyond the barrier, a group of Hitler Youth were laughing and cracking jokes.

The people behind the barrier seemed subdued; I didn't hear one word of approval. A woman beside me said she'd been at the Stadtwald and seen Jews being hauled away in trucks. A man said he'd just come from Friedberger Anlage; there, too, the synagogue was burning, and so was the old synagogue on Alkerheiligenstrasse.

The round synagogue building was burning like a torch. There were two fire engines right next to it. One had a big ladder but it hadn't been extended. The other carried equipment. Some firemen were standing around with hoses, but they weren't fighting the blaze, only spraying the pieces of burning wreckage that fell to the street. Obviously they had orders to let the synagogue burn and just to stop the fire from spreading to the buildings around it.

I don't remember how long I stood there, staring at the flames. I had a feeling I'd never known before. I felt that I was one of these humiliated and tormented people. I'd never realized so fully how much I was one of them. These people, whose windows were being smashed, whose homes were being ransacked, their shops demolished, their synagogues destroyed, their scrolls of the Torah desecrated, these people who were being tortured and killed were my brothers and sisters. Their fate was my fate; I, too, was one of the chosen people, certainly not among the bravest and noblest, or most pious, but one of them all the same, no matter how many lies we told. Nor at that moment did I want to lie my way out of it.

I knew that most of the people around me felt no horror at the sight of the burning synagogue, but I didn't hate them. To them it was a big show—the kind of thing that gives you gooseflesh for a while. I was very sad; it seemed to me that someone ought to say the *Shema Yisroel* aloud, a last profession of faith before the end. Suddenly I heard Papa's voice singing the mournful revolutionary old song that he sometimes sang at home, by himself or with Mama—I haven't heard anyone sing it since, I suppose it's been forgotten:

> *Hulet, hulet, beyze Vindn,*
> *yetz iz ayer Zait,*
> *lang vet doieren der Vinter,*
> *Zummer iz noch vait.*

> *Raisst die Loden fun die Fenster,*
> *Shaiben brecht arois,*
> *brennt a Lichtl ergets Finster,*
> *lesht mit Zorn es ois.*

> *Yogt de Feygl fun die Velder,*
> *vait fertraibt zey fort,*
> *die vos kennen nit mehr flihen,*
> *toit zain oif dem Ort.*

> *Howl, howl angry winds*
> *This is your season,*
> *The winter will be long,*
> *Summer is still far off.*

> *Tear the shutters from the windows,*
> *Blast out the panes,*
> *If light is burning somewhere in the darkness,*
> *Put it out with your fury.*

> *Drive the birds out of the forest,*
> *Scatter them far and wide,*
> *Those that cannot flee*
> *Can only drop dead.*

There were hundreds of people, but all I could see was flames and smoke, and Papa's soft, sad voice sounded in my ears as if he were standing right behind me: *"Hulet, hulet, beyze Vindn."* He was so close I'd only have to turn around to see him. And in my head the refrain echoed: *"Lang vet doieren der Vinter, Zummer iz noch vait."* The tears ran down my cheeks, and I didn't care if anyone were watching me or not.

Slowly I went back to the office. No one asked me where I'd been. Half an hour later the Hitler Youth member came in. His face and hands were covered with grime.

"What's new?" the others asked him.

"What's new? Do I have to tell you?"

No. But he told us all the same. His platoon leader had alerted him the previous afternoon; an action was being planned for the night and his unit should stand by. They'd woken him at three in the morning, and half an hour later he was at the meeting place in the North End. Hundreds of Hitler Youth members had been present. They'd been broken down into groups and then they had set out for the inner city by different routes. Each group had systematically smashed the windows of the Jewish stores in the street assigned to it, broken and gutted the interiors. Then they had burst into the homes of Jews, forced them to leave, smashed the windows, and thrown the furniture out into the street.

The streets were strewn with glass; that's why that pogrom came to be known as Crystal Night.

The people who'd been driven out of the houses were rounded up by storm troopers and led away.

The Hitler Youth member was coming to the end of his story. "We caught one kike and clipped his beard and ear locks. He looked like a beet when we got through with him. You'd have died laughing. His eyes were popping out of his head like a frog."

An older man asked, "I suppose they beat them too?"

"What do you mean by that?" the squad leader asked.

"Nothing at all. You know how people talk."

"I guess you feel sorry for them?"

The man didn't answer. The Hitler Youth member turned away, offended at the lack of applause. Later on he came over to me at my drawing board, to tell me more about his heroic deeds. His group had been sent to the synagogue on Friedberger Anlage. A truck loaded with jerry cans full of gasoline was already waiting across the street. Oh, yes, the preparations had been made well in advance. They poured the gasoline into the building through the open doorway and the shattered windows, and kindled it with soaked rags. But it didn't take the first time, and they had to repeat the operation twice more before the building went up in flames.

I stood at my drawing board and tried to look indifferent. But he must have noticed something about my expression, for he broke off his story and said, "This doesn't interest you, does it?"

"Frankly, no."

"Do you like the Jews?"

What could I say? One lie more or less meant nothing to me. I'd been lying ever since I could remember. But at that moment I couldn't manage it. "Whether I like Jews or not is neither here nor there. But this much I'll tell you. I'm sick of your stories. In my opinion what was done to the Jews today was unjust; it was un-Christian."

The Hitler Youth leader was flabbergasted. He glared at me for a moment, then he hissed, "And you call yourself a German!"

"Leave me alone," I said, and turned back to my drawing board.

But he didn't leave me alone. "Go on, say some more. I'm curious to know what else is on your mind."

I saw that I'd gone too far.

"For your information," he said, taking an official tone, "I'll have to report what you've just said. It's my duty."

That afternoon Herr Bernhardt, our boss, called me into his office. The Hitler Youth leader was sitting there.

"Herr Senger," said the boss, "I'm told that you made

certain remarks about the events of last night. Is that true?"

"I only said . . ."

He cut me off sharply. "I already know what you 'only' said. I will not tolerate agitation against the government or the party in my enterprise. Get that through your head. Have you anything to say? Very well. Take this as a warning. You may go."

It could have been a lot worse. I only hoped the Hitler Youth leader would let it go at that. He spent the rest of the day in the office and that reassured me a little, because if he was right there, he couldn't be running to the party or the Gestapo—not for the moment at least.

Half an hour later Herr Bernhardt called me back. This time he was alone. "Sit down," he said. His voice was different, friendlier than before. "I hope," he said, "you realize how stupid you've been. In times like these you can't just go shooting off your mouth. I've decided to transfer you to the Riederwald plant. Is that satisfactory?"

"Yes, sir. Of course."

Actually I was delighted. Working practically on top of that Hitler Youth member would have been an unbearable strain, for I knew he'd always be on the lookout for another opportunity to denounce me, probably to the party next time. And then I'd really be sunk.

"Your colleague would give you no peace," Herr Bernhardt went on. "Yes, you'll be better off in Riederwald." He stood up to indicate that the interview was at an end. But then he said something I wouldn't have expected because he had always professed loyalty to the Hitler regime. "Everyone is entitled to his own opinion of what happened in Frankfurt today. But one keeps it to oneself. That's what I wanted to say to you. And now get back to work."

Herr Bernhardt "did his duty" during the whole Hitler period; he was a reliable factory manager, and held out to the bitter end. The Hitler Youth leader volunteered for the army and died at Stalingrad in 1943.

The day of horror wasn't over yet. Late that evening Dr. Zely Hirschmann's sister Erika, who worked as a secretary for the Israelite community* brought us bad news. The Jewish Welfare Agency on Königswarterstrasse had been raided by the SA. They had ransacked all the rooms, arrested the staff, and made off with a card file containing the names of all the people who had ever received assistance. Anyone who perused that file would be sure to come across our name. And the records of the Israelite community on Fahrgasse, including the membership file, had also been confiscated. There too our name was listed, though we had withdrawn from the Jewish community years before.

Our whole family agreed that this was the end when we discussed it later among ourselves. We only worried about what would happen to Sergeant Kaspar if someone studied the card file of inhabitants at the Hochstrasse police station and discovered that the religious affiliation on our card had been changed.

That some day we would come to the end of this road was something we'd accepted long since. But the uncertainty about when the time would come had grown to an almost intolerable burden. So we waited calmly, almost serenely, for the fatal knock on the door. We waited two, three, four days. Mama was having her heart seizures, and I was plagued by stomach cramps. We waited for weeks and months. But nothing happened.

*Up to November 1938 there existed in Frankfurt an "Israelite religious community" and a nonreligious "Israelite community." By order of the Gestapo the two were merged into a "Jewish community." Today there is only one "Jewish community."

A Visit to the Doctor's

My stomach cramps had become unbearable. I writhed and groaned, massaged my belly, or plied it with hot compresses until it looked like a boiled lobster. Nothing helped. I'd have to go to the doctor's if only to get a prescription for painkillers. I had no choice.

Mama was aghast when I told her. She was sure the doctor would notice that I was circumcised and start asking questions. Papa and Paula and Alex were worried too, but in the end we all realized that I couldn't go on living in such agony. So the family council finally consented to my seeing a doctor. Up until then neither Papa nor Alex nor I had ever needed one, so we hadn't stopped to consider the problem. As usual it was Mama who thought up a solution. You've got to admit it was brilliant even if it wasn't very realistic. In the days when Mama lived in southern Russia there had been quite a few Skoptsy in the region. The Skoptsy were a forbidden sect, founded in the seventeenth century. At the start they had the horrible custom of mutilating themselves to atone for their supposed share of original sin. Then in the course of time the mutilation became purely symbolic and took the form of circumcision.

While I groaned and dug my fists into the pit of my stomach, Mama taught me my lesson. "Listen carefully, Valya, here's what you're to tell the doctor in case he asks about your circumcision. Your parents are Volga Germans; they used to be Skoptsy, so they went in for circumcision and that's why you're circumcised. If the doctor wants to know more, tell him it was done right after you were born, in some Frankfurt hospital. That's your story, don't you say one word more. Understand?"

I learned my story by heart. It didn't seem very plausible to me, but you didn't argue with Mama. What for? To make her unhappier than she was already?

We looked up specialists for digestive ailments in the classified directory and found a Dr. Kurt Hanf-Dressler. Mama remembered that Frau Volk in the front building had consulted him and spoken well of him. His office was on Blittersdorfplatz, and that wasn't far away.

My family saw me off as if I were going to Australia. The fifteen-minute walk down Mainzer Landstrasse seemed endless. My heart was beating like a triphammer, but my stomach cramps were gone for the first time in days. I thought of turning around, but I knew the pains would come again. So I kept going.

There were about twenty people in the doctor's waiting room, leafing through magazines and looking bored. I was relieved to see so many. I figured my turn wouldn't come for at least two hours, maybe three. My stomach pains were really gone. The patients seemed to be filing in much too fast. Now there were only five ahead of me. The door opened, but instead of the nurse, the doctor himself stood in the doorway, calling the next patient in. Under his white smock he was wearing the uniform of the SA, the storm troopers. Up above I could see his brown shirt collar with some insignia of rank on it, and down below I saw breeches and riding boots. Later on I found out that Dr. Hanf-Dressler was an officer in the mounted SA. The only sensible thing for me to do was to beat it. There was still time, no one would have stopped me. I've often wondered why I just sat there with my fellow patients, leafing through tattered old magazines. Maybe I was paralyzed by fear. I heard the SA doctor moving about and talking in the next room. I counted the patients ahead of me, three, two—and waited to be called.

Then I sat across the desk from him telling him about my complaint. Dr. Hanf-Dressler listened, without much interest it seemed to me, jotted down a few notes, put away a file card. Then he said, "Now unbutton your shirt and lie down on the table over here."

I complied. He bent over me. All I could see was the twin insignia on his brown shirt with the silver stars, it was as if two wicked little eyes were glaring at me. He ran his fingers over my stomach, pressing here and there, and located the focus of pain between my ribs. Then he palpated my abdomen.

"Does it hurt here?"

"No."

"Here?"

"No."

"Unbutton your trousers."

I fiddled clumsily with the buttons and he pulled my trousers down, as he must have done hundreds of times. "Well, well, what's this?"

"I beg your pardon?"

"Are you circumcised?"

"No . . . yes."

"No . . . yes. What does that mean?"

I stammered something about the Skoptsy, who felt so guilty about their share in the world's original sin that they used to castrate themselves. "And that's why my parents had me circumcised."

"Rubbish!" he said. "How can you talk such nonsense?

You were born right here in Frankfurt, weren't you? Who performed the operation?"

"It was done in a hospital."

"If a medical doctor had done it, it would look entirely different. Who do you think you're talking to?"

"But, doctor, I assure you . . ."

He interrupted me. Now he seemed really exasperated. "Let's not have any more of that. This is a Jewish ritual circumcision and any doctor would recognize it at a glance." And after a long silence: "Never tell that story again." Then he went on palpating me. "Does it hurt here?"

"No."

"Here?"

"No."

He yanked my trousers up, went to the sink, washed his hands, and said, "You can get dressed. Your stomach trouble seems to be of nervous origin. Possibly there's just a trace of gastritis, inflammation of the mucous membrane of the stomach. I'm going to prescribe a 'rolling cure.' "

He sat down at his desk, wrote out a prescription, told me what not to eat, and how to give myself a rolling cure. He dismissed me with the words: "If it doesn't get better, you'll just have to come back. Goodbye, Herr—" he looked at my card—"Herr Senger."

He took me to the outer door, opened it for me, and said to his nurse, "Call in the next patient," and returned to his examination room. The door closed behind him.

Again I expected disaster. Every member of the SA swore a solemn oath to serve Hitler and the Third Reich, to combat the Marxists and Jews and safeguard the purity of the Aryan race. It was the duty of SA officer Dr. Hanf-Dressler to report a crypto-Jew. And it was only too obvious that he had identified me as a Jew—unmasked me, so to speak.

And that wasn't all. By that time—it must have been toward the end of 1938 or early in 1939—all Jews were required by law to use a distinguishing first name, "Sarah" for women and "Israel" for men, on all official documents, passports, identification papers, medical certificates, and so on. A glance at my medical certificate would have told the doctor that I hadn't registered as a Jew for it bore only my right name, the "Israel" was lacking.

In other words I was leading an illegal existence, a fact that medical secrecy could hardly excuse him from reporting, since the absence of the name Israel had little or no connection with my stomach trouble.

I didn't tell my parents what had happened. What was the use? Mama would only have another heart attack, and Papa would put cold compresses on her chest, pace the floor, and moan, "O God, what have we done to deserve this?"

Alex was the only one I told. He was convinced that Dr. Hanf-Dressler would report us. So was I. We waited for the ax to fall. After days of uncertainty it became clear to me that the doctor had kept my secret, so saving our family from deportation and death.

Years later, I found out that Dr. Hanf-Dressler, though a member of the mounted SA, had helped any number of Jews. In spite of the law he had given them medical treatment outside of office hours; he had even hidden a Jewish couple in his hunting lodge in Spessart for more then six months, until an opportunity arose of smuggling them across the border; and until his private clinic in the West End of Frankfurt was destroyed by American bombers, he had employed a Jewish woman doctor there as a nurse under an assumed name.

After the war Dr. Hanf-Dressler worked in the provinces and did not return to Frankfurt until some time in the fifties. In 1967 I heard just by chance that he was chief physician at the Bürger hospital. I decided to go and see him, remind him of our previous meeting, and thank him.

But I hesitated, I thought he might misunderstand me. My wife urged me to go. We spoke of it for the last time at the end of 1970. I promised faithfully to call up and make an appointment. Early in February 1971 I phoned the hospital. His secretary told me he was off on a vacation and I should call again in two weeks.

A few days later I read in the *Frankfurter Rundschau* that Dr. Kurt Hanf-Dressler, chief physician of the Bürger hospital, and his wife, had been killed by an avalanche while skiing in the Silvretta region of Austria. He had died on his sixty-seventh birthday.

When in Doubt, Do Nothing

After I'd passed my apprentice's examination, Remy Eyssen, the director of the firm, called me in and asked me when I was planning to leave. His impatience was understandable. The situation of the Jews had got steadily worse in the year that had passed since Crystal Night. In addition to all sorts of economic penalties imposed on him, a Jew was now obliged to carry a card identifying him as such, stamped with a big "J" and bearing the name of Sarah or Israel. All Jewish children were barred from attending German schools. And any German caught helping or in any way shielding a Jew could expect a long prison term.

Remy Eyssen was in a tight spot. Every new anti-Semitic regulation and every increase in penalties for helping Jews increased his danger. He was horrified when I told him I didn't know exactly when I'd be leaving the company.

He bent over his desk and leaned toward me. "What do you mean, you don't know? Wasn't it agreed between us?"

"Yes, it was," I answered, embarrassed. "But certain things have changed since then."

"What has changed? Isn't Palestine where it was a year ago?" He hadn't meant to say that. The words had just slipped out. I could see he was sorry. He'd never said anything about my being a Jew. "I wanted to help you," he said a little more calmly. "But I'm afraid you've been taking advantage of my good nature." He paced the floor for a few moments, looking down as though deep in thought. Then he said, "You may go now."

I crept away. I felt very guilty. Even if I had thought seriously of going to Palestine, it was too late now; any steps I took would only bring ruin on my whole family. Merely by neglecting to register as Jews we had broken half a dozen laws. An application for permission to emigrate would uncover all our subterfuges. And even the formalities involved in changing jobs would have had the same effect.

Whatever Remy Eyssen did, he was running a risk. In the end he did the most decent thing, the most dangerous for him and the best for me: nothing. He kept me on but sent me back to the Sachsenhausen plant, where I'd at least be out of his sight.

There I had the good fortune to make contact with some fellow workers who hated Hitler and the Third Reich as much as I did. It cost me quite some trouble to sniff out their political opinions and win their confidence.

In the end there were seven or eight of us. We'd meet regularly to exchange information and discuss the events of the day. We had created a small anti-Fascist cell. One of the members was Bernhard Fröhlich, the head of the crane-and-hoist department; another was a young engineer who worked under him. The department secretary was one of us, too, so we could talk freely in her presence. Then there was Heinz Kreuter, one of the gatekeepers, an older man; two workers on heating installation duty; and a heating technician who had taken his apprentice's examination along with me and who remained my friend for years; from 1940 on there was Irmgard Dröll, who was to play an important part in my life later on.

Whenever I think of the Sachsenhausen plant, where I worked until 1944 and even rose to be a department head, I remember two incidents that could easily have sealed my doom. They show the strange state of mind I developed. I became so accustomed to danger that I forgot all about it, and imagined for long periods of time that I could relax and live like other people. Perhaps that helped us to survive.

The introduction of rationing for tobacco and cigarettes confronted me with a serious problem. The daily ration came to ten cigarettes at first; later it was reduced to five and then three. Being a heavy smoker, I was forced to buy from non-smokers or on the black market, in both cases at exorbitant prices. As the ration shrank, the black-market price went up. In the end it was four or five times the legal price—if you were lucky enough to have a source.

"Black" Thekla was the owner of a cigar store on Schulstrasse. I'd known her for years, so I could always count on her for cigarettes; the only problem was financial, for with Thekla business was business, and I had to pay the black-market price like everybody else.

One day I had an idea. The ration cards had thirty numbers printed on them; but only some of them, which were posted, were good for the purchase of tobacco, cigars, or cigarettes. With the help of eraser, pen, and ink, I thought, it shouldn't be difficult to transform the useless numbers into good ones, for instance a 7 into a 1, a 3 into an 8, an 8 into a 3, a 9 into a 0, and so on. I tried it and submitted a sample to Thekla. It was good clean work, and she went into the risky trade with me. She'd give me small lots of cards that her customers had entrusted to her, and I would change the numbers to coincide with those that had been posted. In return she'd give me a third of the cigarettes she gained through my manipulations. She gave me more and more cards to alter, but we had to wait until the numbers were posted, and then I'd be in a big hurry. So sometimes I'd work on my cards during lunch hour, when I was alone in the drafting room. If someone came in, I'd quickly shove my handiwork under a piece of drafting paper. But one day it was too late. Before I could hide my ration cards, Herr Metz, the chief clerk, was looking over my shoulder. "What's this? Doctoring your cigarette card?"

"No, no, I was only trying . . ."

"Trying?" He pulled out the card and held it up to his nearsighted eyes. "You must be out of your mind! You can be sent to jail for this. Do you want to ruin your whole life for a few lousy butts? Good God, man, leave it alone." He threw the card down on my drawing board. Luckily my fellow draftsmen were out at lunch and nobody could see us.

I spent the next few days in a state of terror. Herr Metz didn't report me, but I'd lost all interest in forging cigarette cards.

A year later I did something no less foolish. One of the workers under me gave me some forged food cards, so-called hotel and restaurant cards, that had been dropped from English planes. The law required me to hand them over to the police. Using them was punishable by death. There must have been about ten sheets of them, indistinguishable from the real ones. But I surrendered only half of them and kept the other half for myself. I even gave two of them to "Black" Thekla in exchange for cigarettes, without telling her where they came from.

In June 1944 my friend and fellow worker Heinz Kreuter married Irmgard Dröll, who belonged to our illegal shop cell. I was very unhappy because I was the one who had converted her to anti-Fascism, and what was more I was in love with her. But Mama's rules had kept me from confessing my feelings to her. I went to the marriage bureau, but only as a witness. That evening, which was memorable for still another reason, we celebrated at a tavern. After the relatives had gone home, our wedding supper turned into a sort of political gathering. At the head of the table sat Pastor Grimm of St. John's Church, who had done time in prison for coming out against euthanasia and the persecution of the Jews; then came the newlyweds, who were both members of our illegal cell, my brother, Alex, who was going with Irmgard's sister at the time, and I, the witness. If the Nazis had known, they'd certainly have sent us to a concentration camp for several decades. We discussed the political situation until long after midnight and agreed that the Third Reich was about to collapse.

Five years later Irmgard *did* become my wife.

That Jewish Smell

I met Lis at the Weilquelle, a tavern at the crossroads between Upper and Lower Reifenberg in the Taunus. She lived in Neu-Isenburg, she and her friend Marga were taking a bicycle trip, and they had stopped into the Weilquelle for lunch. My friend René and I sat down at their table and it didn't take us long to get acquainted. René took a shine to Marga, and I devoted myself to little Lis, who was very lively and entertaining. The girls seemed to like us, and we spent a pleasant afternoon together.

Later we invited Lis and Marga to our weekend cabin in Lower Reifenberg for coffee. René and I spent almost every weekend there, and we had lots of visitors. Sometimes they'd stay overnight. There was a big double-decker bed, the girls would take the lower bunk and the boys the upper.

Lis and Marga had no objection, so we all went to the cabin together. René played the guitar, we sang songs together, and in the evening we all bicycled back to town. From then on, Lis joined us almost every weekend. For me this friendship, confined to walks and bicycle rides and nights in the weekend cabin, had one great advantage, that Mama never could get wind of it. To her mind, every girl I met was a potential menace to the family, something to be resisted tooth and nail.

Lis was a good pal, not the least bit pretentious; she said whatever came into her head, a little too much sometimes. When we were lucky, or when I could arrange it, the two of us would spend a whole night alone in the hut and make love.

When it came to sex, Lis wasn't much more experienced than I, and she had just as little imagination. We made love as best we could, we both enjoyed it, and we were happy. It might have gone on a long time. But it didn't.

Here's what happened. One time we were alone in the cabin. I still remember that Lis had very small breasts, which disappeared entirely when she lay back sated and happy, with her arms folded under her head. Only the nipples, bedded in their dark circles, stood out; they looked like big brown push buttons. So far I hadn't had a chance to sound her out about politics in general and her feelings about the Nazis and their persecution of the Jews in particular. Experienced lovers may say that bed is no place for political discussion. But we had already exchanged all the terms of endearment we could think of and it was natural to change the subject. Anyway, I had no intention of starting a serious political discussion, I only wanted to find out a little more about her, perhaps in the hope of loving her a little more deeply.

The reader should bear in mind that this was in May or June of 1939, when the persecution of the Jews was in full swing. Of the thirty thousand Jews who had lived in Frankfurt only about ten thousand were left. Many had emigrated in time, most had been sent to concentration camps, and those who still remained expected to be deported any day. In addition, war was in the air.

So I asked Lis if she belonged to the League of German Girls, and I was glad when she said no. She added that she wasn't interested in politics and assured me she had nothing against Jews. That made me even gladder and I gave her a little squeeze. Then she said something very sensible.

"I think it's the same with the Jews as with us, there are good ones and bad ones. I even had a Jewish girl friend. She and her family went to America. And a good many of the customers of our nursery garden were Jews."

"Then you have nothing against the Jews?"

"No. I've already told you that."

I gave her another squeeze.

"But there's one thing I've noticed about Jews, Vali. They're an entirely different race, you can't get around it. They're different from us."

My curiosity was aroused. "Different?" I asked. "In what way?"

"In every way. They way they act, the way they move, and especially the way they smell."

"The way they smell? What do you mean?"

"If you had known as many Jews as I have, you'd know what I mean."

"Tell me some more."

"It's perfectly simple. Rich or poor, young or old, male or female, they all have the same nasty smell, that typically Jewish smell."

In that moment our love began to stink in my nostrils. Lis continued, "If your nose were as sensitive as mine, you could pick out a Jew from among a hundred Christians."

When I told her I was feeling sick, she was genuinely worried about me. I climbed up on the upper bunk and spent the night alone. I don't believe she ever realized why I broke with her.

Rosa

During the war, the blackout was a big help to me; it enabled me to slip unnoticed from Trierische Gasse through the big arch into Vogelsgesanggasse, the street where the whores hung out. The darkness made it almost impossible to recognize the men lined up along the walls.

Now and then a door opened, a faint beam of light fell on the front steps and a few square yards of the cobbled street, and the shadow of a man would flit across it into the darkness. Or else there'd be whispering and haggling in a doorway, and a shadow would vanish into the house.

Many a night I'd gone to one of these streets, but I'd seldom ventured into the narrow strip of light, discussed the price, and followed the girl upstairs.

One night late in the summer of 1941 I was loitering on Vogelsgesanggasse, not daring to approach any of the prostitutes. I saw a woman coming down the street, swaying slightly. When she was about ten feet away from me, a man detached himself from the wall and went toward her. Probably someone like me, a prospective customer. Later, she claimed it was her pocketbook he was after. Anyway, when the man came up to her, she recoiled, shouted "Beat it, you punk" or something of the kind, and stumbled. She grabbed hold of me for support, swore, and reached for her shoe that had fallen off. The man had disappeared in the meantime.

For me this was a golden opportunity, and I took advantage of it. I picked up the little bouquet she had dropped, and her shoe, which had a button or buckle missing. While helping her hobble down the street on one shoe, I asked if I could go upstairs with her.

"Not tonight, son. Can't you see I'm too stinko? Come tomorrow, just ask for Rosa."

That's how I met Rosa. When I arrived the following night, she sent me away, but told me to come back in an hour, when the last of her customers would be gone.

I came back and she took me to bed with her. She didn't treat me at all the way the girls usually treated a paying customer, just lifting her skirt and opening up her blouse. We took all our clothes off, except a little sleeveless vest that Rosa kept on because she had a slight cold. I remember that night well. We sat up in bed smoking a cigarette, and Rosa told me about her thirteen-year-old daughter, who was in boarding school somewhere in Franconia. She had no idea what her mother was doing in Frankfurt, and Rosa was determined that she should never find out.

When that subject was exhausted, Rosa told me about her birthday. She and some girl friends had had a few drinks to celebrate it the night before, that's why she'd been so plastered. Almost apologetically she said, "I got to admit it, I sop it up, but I don't very often get drunk." Then, after a while: "Are you clean, kid? No clap? Good, then we don't need a rubber. A rubber spoils it. Let's have a look." She pressed the tip of my penis and deftly pulled back the skin. "Say," she exclaimed. "You got a Jewdickey."

I must have turned green, and I suppose she noticed,

because before I could say anything, she said reassuringly, "It don't matter. I don't care what you are." And she gave me a friendly pat on the cheek.

It was an exciting and eventful night. Rosa was an excellent teacher and I was an eager pupil. In addition, her good humor was contagious, and she was a really remarkable storyteller, a Scheherazade of the red-light district. Before 1933 she had plied her trade in Nuremberg. An astonishing number of her customers had been Jews—that was probably for my benefit, because they'd all been fine decent men, who never demanded disgusting "specialties." Since 1933 things had been different. She told me about the times when she and a handpicked group of "colleagues" would be rounded up and taken to the Deutscher Hof to entertain high Nazi leaders. Half the time they'd get the supermen drunk and take them for all they were worth. What she told me in one night about the life of a whore was a veritable *Decameron* laced with a strain of *Fanny Hill.*

There was a bottle of cognac on the floor beside the bed and we'd take a nip now and then, nor did we neglect the main activity. Rosa told more and more stories. It got late, very late, and she was still talking. She asked me to stay all night. She didn't know that Mama was waiting for me—and how she was waiting!

I don't remember what lie I told her to get away, obviously I couldn't tell her the truth. Rosa was annoyed with me, but only because she had to get up and go downstairs to let me out. It must have been three or four in the morning. I ran all the way home. My hand was trembling as I turned the key in the lock.

*

Even if my key had been made of cotton, you'd have heard me, Mama. You couldn't help hearing, you hadn't slept a wink all night, you'd been sitting up in bed waiting for me, three pillows at your back.

You came into the living room in a sleeveless flannel nightgown. You wept and you moaned, you wrung your hands and asked God what you'd done to deserve this. And then Papa, stooped over as usual, came from the bedroom in his long underdrawers. He hadn't shut an eye either. He didn't say anything, but his gestures underlined every one of your outcries, and he shook his head over his unnatural son. Finally, Mama, you said what you'd said so often: *"Oy oy oy,* you'll be the end of us yet!"

But what would you have said if you'd heard Rosa exclaim about my "Jewdickey"!

You sank into a chair exhausted. It was more than your poor sick heart could bear. Papa shuffled off to the kitchen and came back with a wet towel, which you maneuvered through the décolleté of your nightgown and placed under your left breast.

I felt wretched. Maybe you were right, Mama. Maybe it was true that I thought only of myself and my pleasure. Of course it was wrong of me to do things that put you and Papa and Alex and Paula in danger. I'd have liked to stroke your gray hair, Mama, but I didn't dare.

*

In those days a Jew had no business thinking about his sexual needs. I knew it even then, and I felt thoroughly ashamed of myself. But no amount of shame could make my needs go away.

Three nights later I crept back to Vogelsgesanggasse to breathe her fragrance; she smelled of musk and roses, of nutmeg and cheap perfume, of fish, salt, and earth.

Rosa was always glad to see me. She always had some new story to tell. "My little Jewdickey" became her favorite term of endearment. One night I felt sure enough of her affection to ask her, "Well, suppose I was one?" And she answered, "Who you trying to kid? I've known it all along, so what. Just keep it to yourself."

That was all, she never mentioned the matter again, and neither did I. And that's why I'm writing about Rosa now.

One night when I came to see her, she was terribly depressed. Someone had written to the principal of her daughter's school, calling her attention to Rosa's profession. I believed every word of Rosa's story. I'd have thrashed anybody —if I'd been capable of thrashing anybody—who cast doubt on it. She said she was trembling for fear the principal might tell her daughter and her daughter would reject her. Then she cried so hard the tears came to my eyes too.

She was inconsolable. "What wicked people there are in the world."

The end of our acquaintance was as unusual as the beginning. Rosa was arrested. Late one afternoon two policemen came to Vogelsgesanggasse and took her away, barely leaving her time to throw a few clothes and toilet articles into a suitcase. I heard about it that night from her neighbors. Such arrests were common enough at a time when people were disappearing every day. Unregistered prostitutes were sent to labor camps and homosexuals to concentration camps.

But why had Rosa been arrested? I was afraid to ask questions on Vogelsgesanggasse and I still have no idea. I never saw her again.

It was a relief to Mama, because I took to spending more time at home.

How fervently I wish Rosa had managed to come through the Hitler period unscathed. How I wish that every time she was tired and her nose itched she'd have a man's stubbly cheek to scratch it on and fall asleep mumbling unintelligible words as she did with me.

Sometimes, I think: Mustn't Rosa be counted among the resistance to the Nazi regime?

The parents. Berlin, approximately 1907.

The family, 1926. From left to right: Papa, Alex, Paula, Valentin, Mama. Frankfurt.

No. 12 Kaiserhofstrasse.

"Fressgasse" or "Swill Street."

*Crystal Night, November, 8, 1938:
The synagogue on Börneplatz burning.*

1942.

Paula,

Alex,

and Valentin.

Transport of Jews to
Theresienstadt on
August 18, 1942.

Downtown Frankfurt, 1944.

*View from the window of
No. 12 Kaiserhofstrasse,
toward "Fressgasse."
Taken in 1965, before the
building was torn down.*

Valentin Senger on Kaiserhofstrasse, 1978.

Mimi—An Interim Love

She was eight years older than I, but many years richer in experience. She was small, plump, and affectionate. Her freckled face radiated friendliness, there always seemed to be a smile on it. She loved music and had a fine voice. She especially liked to sing Leoncavallo's *Matinata* and the tears came to her eyes when the two of us struck up Richard Strauss's *All Souls:* "Put the fragrant mignonette on the table, bring in the last asters, and let us talk of love, as long ago in May, as long ago in May."

She radiated sexuality, and like all the sexy women I've known, she was lavishly generous, with her love, her money, and everything else.

She came of a family of carnival people from Sauerland. One of her brothers, she told me with pride, owned an autodrome, a scenic railway, and a Ferris wheel, which put him in the upper middle class among carnival people.

The rest of her family, brothers, uncles, and aunts, spent the summer doing the fairs in the territory between the Ruhr and the Sieg. The equipment consisted of two or three shooting galleries, some swings, a rudimentary merry-go-round, and a rather pathetic-looking Ferris wheel.

We got to know each other in a small illegal group that was organized in 1938. Mama and Papa belonged to it at first, because after Crystal Night their Jewish cell had folded; it had dissolved on its own after some members left the country and others had been arrested.

The whole group knew who we Sengers really were, but no one worried about our being an additional risk. As for me, I regarded membership in an illegal group neither as an adventure nor as an additional burden on top of the oppressive situation at home. On the contrary, the companionship of these like-minded people made me feel sheltered and put me at my ease. For a few hours I could drop my mask and be myself.

Though we were definitely a political group, our underground work didn't amount to much. Our principal activity was celebrating revolutionary occasions, May 1, or the anniversary of the murder of Karl Liebknecht and Rosa Luxemburg, or November 9, the date of the October Revolution in Russia, that kind of thing. Our arrangements were always the same: Franz, Mimi's brother-in-law, delivered an "ideological" speech, then Mary, his wife, declaimed a poem relevant to the occasion by Vladimir Mayakovsky or Erich Weiner, and I would read one of my own poems. At the end we'd all hum the "Internationale," because singing would have made too much noise, and then with tears in our eyes and a catch in our throats, we'd break up.

There was no great risk in the Marxist study sessions in Franz's apartment or the information meetings at our place or Lotte's; it was only when we tuned in on the German-language broadcasts of Radio Moscow that my pulse would speed up.

During the first year or two there'd be a bit of excitement when Franz received a small package containing copies of an illegal paper we were supposed to distribute, or on the nights when Mimi and I would paste two homemade anti-Hitler posters on lampposts. We didn't do it very often. And once in a while, we'd stuff leaflets into mailboxes.

During the war, when the blackout made such activities a little easier, Mimi hit on the idea of putting up bigger posters with more than one sentence written on them. We tore two sheets out of a school copybook and daubed them with India ink. In addition to "Down with Hitler," there'd always be another sentence. I don't remember the exact wording, but the whole text was short enough for a person to read in passing, because no one would dare to be seen stopping in front of an anti-Hitler poster. We attached tape to the four corners and rolled up the two pages.

It wasn't easy to find a suitable place. One place I thought of was the East Station, which was always full of commuters in the morning, people who worked in the eastern factory district of Frankfurt. If we could put up our two little posters there during the night, a lot of people would see them the next day.

I reconnoitered the station inside and out and found two suitable spots, a side door leading to the toilets from the south entrance, and a wooden fence on the north side. I worked out a technique: on my way out of the toilet, it would take me only a couple of seconds to paste one of the posters on the swinging door. Then I'd make a quick circuit of the station and fasten the second poster to the fence on the north side, where hardly anyone passed at night. If there was time enough, I could secure it with thumbtacks. At half-past eleven, half an hour before the last train left, there wouldn't be anyone in the station. That would be the best time.

Everything went off as planned. I was scared stiff the whole time, I knew the risk I was running. The first poster was already on the door and I'd just pasted the second on the fence. No one had noticed me. I fished the thumbtacks out of my coat pocket.

Then I heard a voice behind me. "Hey you! What do you

think you're doing?" I turned around. There were two railroad policemen behind me. I hadn't heard them coming. While one leaned forward to read the poster, the other grabbed me by the arm. "All right," he said. "Let's go."

I wrenched myself free. There was a grass plot outside the station and I ran straight across it in the pitch-darkness. I ran for dear life.

I don't know how long those railroad policemen followed me. I didn't look around, I just kept running, around one corner and then another. Suddenly I saw I was on Habsburger Allee. It was just before midnight. Mimi lived two hundred yards farther on, on Brüder-Grimm-Strasse. If I could get to her place, I'd be safe. I looked behind me for the first time. There wasn't a soul in sight. I had shaken off my pursuers.

I climbed over the garden gate, slipped into the laundry room, which was never locked, and out the other end to the stairwell. I was shaking like a leaf, my teeth were chattering, I had to sit down on the stairs. My stomach cramps started up again.

Frau Hermann, Mimi's landlady, must have heard me. She opened the door and saw me sitting there. Luckily she knew me. Startled, she asked if she could help me or if she should go and get Mimi. I mumbled something about my heart, and dragged myself up the stairs, clinging to the banister.

Mimi put hot cloths on my belly and sat beside me on the couch. I wanted to tell her what had happened, but she stopped me. "Better rest first. You'll tell me later."

I lay on Mimi's couch in the kitchen-living room and didn't feel the least bit heroic. It was just plain stupid to risk our own lives and those of several other people with such useless foolishness. What drove me to play the hero? Strange as it may seem, the answer is cowardice. I was too cowardly to say no when Mimi said something had to be done all the time to show the people that there were still Communists and anti-

Fascists in Germany, that someone was resisting the Nazis. I was too cowardly to say no, though even then I knew the futility of what we were doing. Quite a few of our comrades had been arrested and sent to concentration camps for the same sort of nonsense, and many of them had never come back.

And there was still another reason, I think, for my playing the hero in spite of my fear: it was my way of rebelling against Mama. For years she had drummed it into me that our only chance of survival was to keep quiet, to cringe, and do nothing. For fear of exposure, she had turned the whole family into cowards, whose first impulse was to hide or to run away from themselves.

When I think of our illegal cell, it's always Mimi who comes to mind first. As far as I was concerned, she was the most important part of the group. Without her, I might have lost interest in underground work; without her, I might have been an even more inept resistance fighter than I was, or none at all. She gave me moral support and gave my activity a certain meaning. And besides, my time with Mimi was a happy time, an important period in my life.

We had both been active in the group for some time before we started sleeping together. She was then twenty-eight and I twenty. She knew my difficulties and helped me to overcome them. Thanks to her, I was able to catch up on a good many things I had missed because of Mama's fears.

With a few interruptions, Mimi and I were together until the end of the war. By the end of summer 1944 our illegal group had ceased to exist; some of its members had been drafted, others had fled from Frankfurt because of the air raids or had been transferred to jobs in less exposed places. We often discussed our future. Mimi spoke of an interim relationship, a marriage of convenience. We agreed that if we were ever released from our political obligations, we should both feel free to go our separate ways.

We were very fond of each other; I don't know if it was

love, but I do know that I was jealous when Mimi took up with other men, which was fairly often, and Mimi was very unhappy about my affair with Ionka, a Bulgarian student. We had our happy times, especially when we took trips together. We both liked to travel.

During one of those periods of happiness we had an adventure that could easily have been the end of me and my family and got Mimi into bad trouble. It was entirely my fault; how I could have been so criminally irresponsible is something I'll never know.

I suppose happiness made me talkative, trusting and giddy; it often did—with Mimi, with Rosa, and with Ionka.

Mama was bitterly opposed to my affair with Mimi. She cursed and reviled her, and scolded me on every possible occasion, calling me an idiot, a gullible fool in the hands of a scheming *shiksa.*

That's how it was in the late summer of 1944, when Paula and I took Mama to the Black Forest, hoping the fresh mountain air would be good for her sick heart. Mimi and I had arranged to meet a few days later in Hinterzarten, as soon as Mama was settled. I told Mama I was planning to take a walking trip all by myself in the Black Forest. Naturally she guessed that Mimi was involved. "So go," she said bitterly. "I don't need you."

I went, but my guilty conscience spoiled the pleasure of being with Mimi. She tried in vain to distract me from my dark thoughts. When nothing helped, she suggested that we should leave Hinterzarten, which was overcrowded with elderly people who'd come for the waters and with wounded soldiers. We decided on a little trip to Lake Constance and left that same day.

I knew that in wartime foreigners were forbidden to go within ten kilometers of the Swiss border, and according to my passport I was a foreigner. I also knew that identity checks were frequent in the border zone. What didn't occur to me was that our route from the Black Forest to Lake Constance would pass through this border zone. Even so, it's likely that nothing would have happened if Mimi hadn't thought of stopping in Singen and climbing the Hohentwiel.

We got off the train in Singen and checked in at the Hotel Sternen near the station. I didn't know that the police were especially vigilant in the area between Thengen and Lake Constance because the hilly, densely wooded country was ideally suited to illegal border crossings. So I wasn't the least bit worried when I handed the desk clerk my foreigner's passport.

We took two single rooms; unmarried couples had to at the time. They were pretty far apart, though on the same corridor. We filled out our registration forms and suspected nothing when the desk clerk said he'd have to keep our papers until he had reported us to the police. And of course we didn't bother to notice which room was assigned to Mimi and which to me.

It was long after midnight when I left Mimi and tiptoed down the corridor to my own room. I was still awake when I heard steps in the corridor. Then someone knocked on a door and a voice said, "Open! Police!"

I didn't dare to look out.

I heard a door closing. Then silence. I wondered if it could have been Mimi's door. But what could the police want with Mimi? I waited with trepidation for the police to go away. Instead, I heard their steps approaching and then came a knocking at my door. I switched on the light and opened. Three men were standing there, one in uniform.

"Police. Are you Herr Valentin Senger?"

"Yes. That's me."

"Then get dressed. You'll have to come with us."

My foreigner's passport had aroused the suspicion of the desk clerk. He had reported my presence to the local police, who had alerted the Gestapo in Constance. Two Gestapo agents had hastened to Singen and a local policeman had guided them to the hotel. The night clerk had given my room number and the three of them had come up to arrest me. But in my supposed room Mimi was sleeping.

When she heard them pounding on her door, Mimi jumped up in a fright. She opened the door and saw three startled faces—they hadn't expected to see a woman. Their first thought was that I must be hiding somewhere. They pushed Mimi aside and searched the room. They lifted the bedspread, looked under the bed and in the clothes cupboard. Finally, one of them asked if she were alone in the room and she truthfully said yes. Then they mentioned my name, and it came to light that we had unwittingly exchanged rooms.

While I was still getting dressed, one of the Gestapo turned to Mimi, who was standing in the door to her room, and commanded, "You come along too."

They took us to the local police station and after an hour's wait drove us to Gestapo headquarters in Constance. There they put us in separate waiting rooms. It was still very early, about six o'clock. At eight Mimi was led out for questioning. Why, the interrogator asked, had we entered the border zone? He was convinced that Mimi had come to help me slip across the Swiss border, and refused to believe her when she said it had been her idea to spend the night in Singen.

He was determined to find out the name of our accomplice, for it was impossible to cross the border unnoticed without the help of someone who knew the region well.

At about nine they brought me in. I had to take my suitcase with me and put it on a table. Two men searched it, picked up every article of clothing and checked for a false bottom. Then one of them frisked me. I was afraid he'd unbutton my trousers, but he didn't.

Then the questions began. Why had I come to Singen? Whom had we been expecting to meet? Didn't I know that foreigners were forbidden to enter the border zone? They didn't seem pleased with my answers, they were getting impatient. I had the impression they'd been hoping to unmask a spy, which would certainly have been more interesting and better for their careers than batting the breeze with someone who wandered into the forbidden zone by mistake. The interrogator brought his open hand down on the table and shouted, "That's enough fairy tales! Out with it! Think we've got all day?"

When I couldn't oblige them and just stuck to my story, they took me back to the waiting room and locked me in. Two hours later they brought me out again. In the meantime, they had been on the phone to Frankfurt. Now they knew all about my family and knew where I worked. I'd have expected that to make them more suspicious than ever. Not at all. Not even my Russian origins seemed to trouble them.

But then something unexpected happened. One of the Gestapo agents left the room and came back with a middle-aged man, who seemed nervous and uneasy.

"Do you know this man?" the Gestapo agent asked, pointing at me.

The man looked at me for a moment and said without hesitation, "No."

"Take a good look."

"No. I don't know him."

The agent took hold of the man's arm and led him away. I never discovered what this confrontation was supposed to accomplish.

At last they said I could go. They returned my passport and gave me strict orders to take the next train out of the border zone.

Mimi was already waiting in the corridor. We looked at each other, and the same thought crossed both our minds: How could we have been so careless?

As if it weren't enough to be a Jew, a Russian-Jewish stateless Communist, to have a false name and a father with a Yiddish accent and a forged passport, and to belong to an illegal political group, I had—just to give Mimi and me a little fun—to register at a hotel in the border zone and throw myself into the arms of the Gestapo.

Half an hour later we were on the train bound for Tuttlingen. But again the line passed through Singen. At Radolfszell a border guard checked our papers. Naturally my foreigner's passport aroused his official suspicions and he dutifully put it in his pocket. He was perfectly friendly but said we'd have to get off at Singen and there he'd make more inquiries.

So there we were back in Singen. This time in the office of the railroad police. We could see the Hotel Sternen two hundred yards away, looking as normal and peaceful as if nothing had happened in the last ten hours. And behind it the Hohentwiel rose into the sky. To this day I haven't climbed it.

The border guard first phoned the local police and then the Gestapo in Constance. Then he smiled, slapped the palm of his hand with my passport, and gave it back to me. "Everything in order. Just get out of here as fast as you can."

We took the next train. We weren't sorry to see the last of Singen.

*

Mama, you were unfair to Mimi, you had no business cursing me tearfully and calling her a whore. She was nothing of the kind. But she was the first woman who laid claim to your son Valya, and she was a *shiksa*. You were politically enlightened, you weren't an Orthodox Jew any more, you were absolutely opposed to all racial prejudice, and yet . . . and yet you held it against Mimi that she wasn't one of our people.

And then there was the frantic fear that made you regard every newcomer to the family as an enemy to be repulsed at all costs. Fear makes people rigid, it makes them tremble and stammer, it prevents them from thinking and destroys their sense of fairness. It was fear that warped your judgment and prejudiced you against Mimi.

Later on, when American planes reduced our section of Frankfurt to rubble and demolished the left half of the back building of No. 12 Kaiserhofstrasse—our apartment was in the right half—you joined the family in fleeing to Mimi's emergency lodgings in Jügesheim. And she took us all in.

Ionka

I'd spent the evening at Mimi's and it was past midnight when
I started home. Mama was waiting for me. She never went to
sleep until we were all under lock and key, and I was usually
the last to get back. All windows were blacked out and there
was no street lighting. What light there was came from a misty
quarter moon. There wasn't a soul to be seen. Since air raids
could be expected every night, people had taken to going to
bed early. I skirted the high brick wall of the Zoological Garden. There it was darker than ever because the dense foliage
of the plane trees shut out the moonlight. I could hardly see
my hand before my face.

Suddenly I had a feeling that I had passed someone in the
darkness. I turned around in a fright and there, pressed against
the wall, was the shadowy form of a woman. All I could actually
see was her face and hands. I stepped closer to her. She made
no move to escape, but rummaged in her handbag and held out
a slip of paper. I took it, but I couldn't read it in the darkness.

"Come with me," I said. I crossed the street and she

followed at a distance. I stopped in a doorway, lit a match
under my jacket, and read what was written on the paper.
"Beethovenstrasse 12."

"That's where you want to go?"

"Yes. I do not know way." She spoke broken German.

"I'm going to Opernplatz. From there it's not far to
Beethovenstrasse."

We walked down the Zeil together. The streetcars had
stopped running two hours before. From time to time I turned
toward her and tried to make out her face in spite of the
darkness.

"Would you like to take a taxi?" I asked.

She shook her head. "No, rather walk."

She was very pretty, about my age, small, delicate face,
smooth, black shoulder-length hair. She could have been Jewish.

I could tell she was inspecting me too. It made me uneasy.
For a while we said nothing, then we talked about the blackout,
the war, and so on.

Little by little I gathered a few facts: she was a Bulgarian,
she'd only been in Germany for three weeks, she'd been a
student at the University of Sofia, she was living with a family
on Beethovenstrasse and doing their housework. It seemed odd
that a student should be working as a housemaid, but I didn't
think any more about it. After a while it turned out that we
could both speak French and that was our best chance of
understanding each other.

In crossing the street, I took hold of her arm to keep her
from stumbling in the darkness. She didn't seem to mind. We
were just coming to Konstabler Wache when the air-raid sirens
blew. I took her by the hand and we ran to the nearest shelter.
For fear of losing her in the darkness, I kept a tight hold on
her hand. It was a pleasure.

We were squeezed tight in the crowded shelter. I could
feel the warmth of her body. Cautiously I put my arm around
her, that way it was much more comfortable on the narrow

bench. She smiled at me. I didn't say a word, I only glanced at her face now and then, and returned her smile. Meanwhile I anxiously watched the uniformed shelter warden, who was striding about with a stern look on his face. Each time he passed, I had the impression that he was scrutinizing the two of us. What if he took the young woman beside me for a forced laborer? Foreign workers weren't allowed to leave their barracks except under guard, and by that time of night they were supposed to be locked in their dormitories. She wasn't dressed at all like the Russian or Polish women in the forced labor gangs, but she had me worried all the same. I kept quiet because I didn't want the shelter warden to hear her talk. Even so, the all-clear signal came a lot too soon.

We walked down the deserted Zeil. We talked a good deal and didn't hurry. Near Hauptwache she bumped into a bicycle that was leaning against a wall; she hadn't seen it in the darkness. She held on to me to keep from falling. Naturally, when we got to Opernplatz, I offered to take her home. The trees on Bockenheimer Landstrasse made it so dark, I said, that I couldn't think of letting her walk there alone. She accepted without hesitation and took my arm. On the corner of Freiherr-vom-Stein Strasse, we kissed for the first time. I began to walk very slowly, because it wasn't far to Beethovenstrasse, and I wanted to feel her there beside me and go on kissing her as long as possible. She told me her name was Ionka Mikhailova Dragova and I could call her Ionka.

We were neither of us eager to part. We sat down on a bench in the little park on Beethovenplatz and pressed close together, because it was a cold March night and we had so much to say to each other. Long after midnight, still on that bench in the park on Beethovenplatz, we made love.

Ionka had come to Nazi Germany of her own free will. In March 1942 that should have aroused my suspicions. She told me she had come to be with a friend who was studying languages at the university. His name was Michael Todorov. She had been with him that very evening. He lived on Am-

Tiergarten, directly behind the zoo. They had quarreled, and Ionka had left him in a fury. She had hardly any money on her, not even enough for a cab.

"Wasn't it lucky I met you!" she said some days later, kissing me.

It was months before I heard the details of her quarrel with Todorov. By then she knew all about me. Love had loosened my tongue and I had put myself in her hands without stopping to think that I was risking my family's safety as well as my own once again.

We continued to make love in that little park. We had nowhere else to go, or so at least I thought. Ionka often asked me if I couldn't find a place where we could be together without having to worry about the elements or about curious night owls. But I could think of no solution. The hotels were closely watched. Though there were some specializing in brief encounters, I didn't know of any. And even if I had, it would have been an unpardonable folly to go there. Mama would never have let us spend the night in our apartment; I wouldn't even have dared to ask her. Once, much later, when we attempted it and Ionka, as prearranged, stayed a little longer than usual, Mama sent her home in no uncertain terms. And Ionka's attic room on Beethovenstrasse was equally unavailable, because I'd have had to pass through her employers' apartment.

We shivered, we got soaked, we were interrupted by every passerby, we were in constant fear of police patrols; one night someone snatched Ionka's handbag with her papers in it; we were always dead tired next day, because we had to wait until everyone else had left the park. And yet, those hours on Beethovenplatz were hours of happiness.

Ionka told me she had broken with her friend. All the same, she knew he had moved to a different apartment and, she found out later that he had gone to Sofia for two weeks to visit his parents.

Naturally I was curious to know where Ionka stood politically, and how she felt about Hitler's Germany. So one day as
we were walking in the Palmengarten, I asked her.

"Tell me, Ionka, do you know who Heinz Beckerle is?"

"Which Beckerle? The one in Sofia?"

"That's right. The German ambassador."

Ionka stopped still. "Why do you ask?"

"Just like that."

"What are you trying to find out?" she asked defensively.

"I thought it might interest you to know that Beckerle
was born and raised in Frankfurt."

"I know."

"How come?" I was surprised. "Do you know him?"

"I've seen him."

"Where?"

"In Sofia, of course. Where else?"

"Did you have dealings with the German embassy?"

"What makes you think that?"

"Your knowing Beckerle."

"A lot of people in Bulgaria know him."

"And knowing he's from Frankfurt."

"That's something I just happened to hear."

Ionka didn't seem eager to talk about Beckerle. But my
curiosity was aroused. So I said, "Beckerle comes of an old
Frankfurt family. He was police commissioner here for years."

She took a few steps in silence. I too was silent. Suddenly
she stood still and said excitedly, "Is there something special
you're trying to find out? Are you trying to test me?"

"Of course not, Ionka."

"That's not the way it sounded."

I was flabbergasted. What could have made her so angry?
Up until then it wouldn't have entered my head to connect her
with Beckerle in any way. I decided to bring up the subject
again some other time. It was a balmy evening, we soon forgot
our bad humor, Ionka was her usual affectionate self again.

Two days later, as we were strolling along the Main, Ionka surprised me by asking, "Valya, how long was Beckerle police commissioner in Frankfurt?"

"From 1933 until the outbreak of the war, I think."

"Then he was in charge of the actions against the Jews?"

"Definitely. As police commissioner, he was responsible."

"For everything?"

"I think so. He was a high-ranking SA leader and the SA was involved in all the actions against the Jews."

"The same as in Sofia," said Ionka. "He brought trouble. I know him all right."

After a while I repeated the question I had asked two days before. "How did you come to know him?"

"Don't ask me that. Oh, Valya, if you knew what terrible things have been happening in Bulgaria!"

She went on to tell me how Bulgaria had changed since 1941, when the German troops had marched in and Beckerle had become German ambassador. He was the sole ruler of the country, the king and the parliament took their orders from him. He persecuted and killed all the patriots and sent the Jews to concentration camps the same as in Germany. Ionka stopped talking and looked at me from the side, as though to study my reaction. "Tell me, Valya. Do you know what they're really doing to the Jews?"

That was a dangerous question to ask at the time. And an even more dangerous one to answer. I answered guardedly, "I think so."

"Isn't it terrible?"

I put my arms around her and kissed her. "I'm glad to hear you say that, Ionka."

"Why?"

"Because now I know we have the same ideas. But you mustn't express such ideas out loud."

"I know that as well as you do, Valya."

"In Germany you've got to be very careful what you say."

"Have I said too much?"

"No. But don't say such things to anyone else. Not to anyone! Understand?"

"I could tell you a lot more, Valya. But you'd be horrified. Or maybe you wouldn't understand."

That night and all next day I thought of what Ionka had said and wondered what more she might have to tell me. It was the first time she had spoken so freely. Up until then she had cut short my attempts to broach the subject. And now this spontaneous confession. That had been careless of her. When I told her so the next day, she said, "I knew I could speak to you, Valya. I trust you."

After that, could I help requiting trust with trust? I kissed her at the streetcar stop, right in the middle of Hauptwache, scandalous behavior which aroused considerable attention in 1942. No words were needed. She caught my meaning.

I took her by the hand, led her across the street, past Katharinenpforte, down Neue Kräme, toward the Main. Near the Paulskirche we were alone. On the big open square no one could come near us without our seeing him first.

Several times I started to speak. Ionka sensed my agitation.

"What's wrong?"

"Nothing. What should be wrong?"

"You're upset, Valya. I can feel it."

I stood still. "You're right. There's something I have to tell you, Ionka."

She took my arm. "Something bad?"

"It's all in how you take it."

"Tell me. No, don't tell me. I don't want to know."

She walked on. I held her back.

"Don't tell me!"

"I've got to. I'm a Jew."

She let go of my arm as if I'd said, "I've got the plague." She took a step backward and stared at me for a moment, then with a strangely toneless voice, she asked, "Is it true?"

"Yes. I'm a Jew."

"It can't be!" She buried her face in her hands and mumbled through her fingers, "It's insane."

I couldn't understand her reaction. Speaking softly, hardly above a whisper, I told her, as far as my halting French permitted, about my family and our situation. The square was deserted. No one passed. Ionka stood still, looking at the ground, and said nothing for what seemed an eternity. Then slowly she raised her head, came back to me, touched me as if she could tell by the feel whether I was really a Jew. "Poor Valya!" she said. Her voice couldn't have been more mournful if she had heard my death sentence.

She had me worried. What was wrong? What had made such a change in her? Did she think there was no hope for me? I took her home. Neither of us spoke on the way. We passed our bench on Beethovenplatz. In parting I asked her, "Do you still love me?"

She didn't answer; she only gave me a hug and disappeared into the house.

After that a shadow hung over our love. We hugged and kissed and made love at night on our bench. But something had changed.

Ionka kept wanting to meet my family, and one day, after impressing it on her that my family must never know that she knew we were Jewish, I took her to Kaiserhofstrasse.

Ionka spoke Russian with Mama and Papa. She stayed for dinner. Mama was already very sick and spent most of the time in bed. Paula and Alex came in later, and Ionka seemed happy for the first time since I had told her I was a Jew.

She came to see us often. She and Mama became good friends. She brought Mama presents, doilies and handkerchiefs she herself had embroidered with Bulgarian folk motifs, a silk purse, an embroidered cushion. But she still seemed sad, and she wasn't as close to me as before. It struck me that she never let me take her all the way home. On Kettenhofweg, or at the farthest on the corner of Westendstrasse, she'd send me away. I often asked if something was troubling her.

"No, nothing," she kept repeating.

One evening when I met her, she was standing there in the street, two suitcases and a hatbox beside her. She told me she had moved out of her room on Beethovenstrasse, but she seemed to be hiding something. My guess was that she had fled.

I said she could stay with us for a few days and offered to ask Mama. No, no, she said, she wouldn't think of it. The idea seemed to frighten her. So we tried the hotels around the Central Station and finally found her a room at the "Vier Jahreszeiten" ("Four Seasons") Hotel.

That night we took a long walk along the Main. For the first time Ionka spoke to me of her family: her invalid father, who had lost a leg in the First World War and was a mere figurehead in the family councils; her severe mother, who hated her father; her elder brother, who had taken a job in Plovdiv chiefly to escape from the constant family quarrels, her other brother, twelve years younger than herself, who was the object of all their mother's love.

Ionka also spoke of her studies. Her life had been hard; her mother, who wanted her to stay home and help with the housework, refused to contribute to her keep at the university, so she had had to support herself with odd jobs. She wanted to become a language teacher. Her French was excellent, and she was proficient in English and Russian.

"We'll go looking for another room tomorrow morning," I said. "And don't worry about the job, we'll easily find you another."

Ionka shook her head. "No," she said. "I won't need a room. I'm going back to Sofia."

I thought I'd heard wrong. "Back to Sofia?"

"Yes. You heard me."

"For God's sake, Ionka, why? And why now?"

No answer.

"Say something. Is there anything I can do?"

She made a gesture of resignation. "No. I have to go, it's the only way. Not on my account, Valya. For your sake. And your family's."

"But there must be some other solution."

"Believe me, there isn't."

"At least we could talk it over."

"You don't understand."

"Then explain."

"It's no use."

I couldn't get anything out of her.

A few days later she asked me to ride out to East Park with her. She wanted to talk to me in a place where we couldn't possibly be overheard.

As we walked hand in hand across the meadow, along the pond and through the gardens, Ionka told me the story of her friend Michael Todorov.

He was the son of a librarian, a quiet studious type with no interest in politics. He had been a student of languages in Sofia when Ionka arrived at the university. They met at lectures and seminars and became friends.

One day during her third term, a student had insulted Ionka. Michael had intervened, the two young men had fought and Michael had wounded his adversary with a knife. Michael was arrested, sent to jail for several months, and expelled from the university.

On his release, he had applied for readmission—in vain. That was in the fall of 1941; by then the Germans had occupied Bulgaria. Someone suggested that Michael should join the League for Germano-Bulgarian Friendship, an organization made up of German officials and Bulgarian collaborationists, for there he would be sure to meet German officials capable of putting pressure on the university authorities.

After some hesitation Michael took his friend's advice and soon became acquainted with a member of the German embassy staff. When he heard of Michael's problem, the German invited him to his office and promised to have Michael reinstated, provided only that Michael agreed to act as an "observer" in an anti-Fascist student group. Michael knew what that meant but accepted. He was determined to go on with his studies, and this seemed the only way.

One day his German contact told Michael that since it would take some time to get him reinstated, he had arranged to send him to the University of Frankfurt for a term. He was to leave the following week.

Michael guessed that his move to Frankfurt was connected with undercover work and he wasn't happy about it. Ionka, in whom he had confided shortly before his departure, agreed with him. But he couldn't refuse. He wasn't even asked whether he wanted to go or not. The German simply gave him a railway ticket and told him what train to take. He was also given a slip of paper with an address on Am-Tiergarten, where a room had already been engaged for him. He was not to report to any German office in Frankfurt; his contacts would come to his room to bring him the necessary papers.

Ionka, who felt partly to blame for Michael's involvement with the Germans, followed him to Frankfurt a short time later. She had hopes of persuading him to give up his espionage work.

Michael had guessed right. He had been sent to Frankfurt for training as an undercover agent. Still, he was allowed to register at the university and study languages. When his contacts found out that Ionka had joined him in Frankfurt, they made him urge her to work for the German secret service at the University of Sofia. That was what they had quarreled about on the night when I bumped into her in the darkness.

Ionka told me all this as we were walking from the pond in East Park through the gardens to Ratsweg Bridge. Night had fallen before she had finished.

"Have you seen much of him since?" I asked.

"I've seen him a few times. It couldn't be helped."

"Do you still love him?"

"No. I haven't loved him for a long time. There's nothing between us. And now, please, please don't ask me any more questions."

She never mentioned him again, neither that night in the streetcar as we rode back to the Central Station, nor in the few days that remained before her departure.

I never found out what had happened, what made her leave Frankfurt in such a hurry, what became of Michael Todorov, and whether or not she herself had been involved with the Gestapo.

Her way of traveling was as strange as her whole story. Instead of buying a through ticket to Sofia, she took the train to Vienna and went the rest of the way by Danube steamer. Apparently she wished to avoid the official border crossing on the railroad line into Bulgaria. But why?

A few weeks later I received a letter from Sofia. Ionka wrote that she had arrived safely and was working in a factory that made uniforms for the Wehrmacht. Then came a terse, impersonal note. And that was the last I heard of her. I wrote several letters, but received no answer.

Whoever she was, she did not denounce me or my family, though she knew all about us. I am convinced that she protected us at the cost of great hardship and danger to herself.

I named my first daughter after her: Ionka.

They Called Him Papichka

Papa was seventy when he went back to his trade. That was in 1940. With millions of men at the fronts and war production in full swing, there was an acute shortage of manpower, and especially of skilled metal workers.

After endless family councils in which we considered the risks, we decided he should apply for a job. He went to the employment office and registered as a skilled turret lathe operator. There were plenty of job offers in spite of his age.

Papa had always been proud of his manual skill. In 1930, during the Depression, he lost his job and had been unemployed ever since. He often spoke of his work. He showed me how to use a slide rule and handle micrometers—the two most important tools of the metal worker—and tried his best to explain the functioning of a turret lathe. He never wearied of telling me how much skill and experience went into the operation of this complicated precision machine. In his day punch-tape-guided automatic and semi-automatic lathes were unknown; everything depended on the craftsman's steady hand

and measuring eye. When something new went into production, it was always Papa who was asked to make the test piece; in pacing the assembly line, the timekeeper always kept his eye on Papa's lathe; and his fellow workers were always asking him to check their pay slips, which he did with the help of a small slide rule. When Papa told me these things, I felt really proud of him. I saw he had gifts that none of us—not even Mama —could equal.

Papa chose a cogwheel factory in Sachsenhausen, a medium-sized plant where he hoped to find good working conditions. At first all went well, the foreman took his age into consideration and gave him time to adjust. But after a while he had to operate two lathes at once like the other machinists and he got paid by piecework. And besides, the foreman began to pick on him and find fault with his work. He was angry at the employment office for not sending him a younger worker and at the factory manager for hiring my father—he had advised him against it—and he took it all out on Papa.

Papa would come home in the evening so exhausted he could hardly eat, so tired he couldn't even read the paper or listen to Radio Moscow.

But his worst problem at the factory wasn't the work; it was his pronunciation. There was no way of avoiding conversation with his fellow workers. When one of them spoke to him, he had to answer. Somebody was always asking him about his strange dialect. If anyone had suspected what it really was and started poking around in Papa's past, or reported his suspicions to some party officer, it would have been the end of him and us all. Because the dialect Papa spoke is not to be found in any part of Germany. It was *mame-loshen,** plain ordinary Yiddish.

Every once in a while someone said to him, "That's a funny dialect you speak. It sounds almost like Yiddish. Where

---

Mame-loshen—mother tongue, from Yiddish *mame* and Hebrew *loshen*, language.

are you from?" Formerly Papa would have said, "We're from Upper Silesia," because he had once been told that his dialect resembled Upper Silesian. But after we dreamed up our ingenious family tree, he said what Mama had told him to say. "We're from the Ukraine. We're Volga Germans."

Still, he wasn't easy about giving himself out for a Volga German. One night he talked about his fear. Suppose a real Volga German happened to be present, then what would he look like? But Mama disagreed. She happened to know that the settlements of Volga Germans were hundreds of miles apart and that different settlements spoke entirely different dialects. How could anyone prove that this peculiar dialect wasn't spoken in some linguistic island in that far-flung region?

It was lucky that no one ever pressed the point and demanded to know where this linguistic island was actually situated. If any Jew had listened to Papa for as much as three minutes, he'd have plucked his sleeve or taken hold of his coat button and said, *"Sengerleben, Ihr rett a gezint Yiddish."**

Up to his death in 1954—blessed be the judge of truth —he spoke with a Yiddish accent, just like any other Jew from the Jewish quarter of Kherson. That in all those years no one ever exposed his German as Yiddish is a miracle. And if you refuse to believe it on the ground that you don't believe in miracles, I won't take it amiss.

It was a big relief for Papa when about six months later the manager took him off piecework and entrusted him with the maintenance and adjustment of the lathes. It also showed that the quality of his work was appreciated.

In the fall of 1942 Papa was seventy-two, and still working as an adjuster at the cogwheel factory in Sachsenhausen. At that time forty Russian women, forced laborers, were assigned to the plant, which was considered essential to the war effort and was therefore given preference in work assignments. At

---

*"Senger, my boy, that's a fine Yiddish you speak."

first a partly disabled mechanic was put in charge of them. His job was to provide for their most urgent needs and teach them the operations they were supposed to perform. But the poor man didn't know one word of Russian. The result was misunderstandings and arguments from morning to night. In the end he couldn't teach them anything.

As was only natural, Papa stepped in as interpreter. But to interpret for forty women, to explain everything under the sun, and straighten out a thousand little difficulties, took too much of his time, and he fell behind in his work. The foreman told him to keep away from the Russian women. The confusion in the machine shop became unbearable.

One day the personnel manager sent for Papa and asked if he'd be willing to devote himself to the Russian women full-time. It might be possible to find another adjuster, but Russian-speaking workers were in short supply. Papa accepted without hesitation. How was he to know that this would be the riskiest adventure of our whole camouflaged existence?

The new job brought a drastic change in his daily program. The women's barracks were on Uhlandstrasse in the East End of town. Every morning at seven Papa had to call for them and escort them to Sachsenhausen on foot, because foreign workers, like Jews, were forbidden to use the streetcars. In the evening he had to take them back again, because they were not allowed on the streets unaccompanied.

Papa's main reason for taking the new job was that he thought he could be of some help to the Russian women, whom he somehow regarded as compatriots and fellow sufferers. Now he'd be doing something more than earning money, he'd have a humane and, as he saw it, a political purpose in life. From little hints he dropped, I gathered that he helped some of them to avoid severe punishment and perhaps even saved their lives.

Most of the women were young. Papa had to keep tabs on their lodging, food, and clothing; he had to teach them the use of the machines, listen to their complaints, and act on those that seemed justified, settle arguments, and accompany his charges on visits to the doctor. Such visits were frequent, because of work injuries, poor food, illness brought on by the cold and the drafty barracks they slept in.

Now and then a Russian woman, who had been accused of one thing or another, such as theft, refusing to work, or "illicit contact" with Germans, would be questioned by the police or the Gestapo. It was always Papa who had to interpret at these sessions and it was very hard on him. The foreman and section heads were quick to report the slightest irregularity; to show "these Russian bitches what the score is," as one of the foremen put it.

My father soon won the women's confidence. They ceased to regard him as a supervisor, he became their "Papichka." They told him everything that was on their minds, and that could be a good deal, enough to make his head spin. His patient explanations put an end to most misunderstandings. Thanks to his influence, their work improved enormously. The management was pleased and gave him a free hand; he was even allowed to decide who should work at what machine, and this enabled him to make life a good deal easier for the women.

But, not satisfied with improving their working conditions, he helped them in many other ways. He would bring them packages of such food as was still available to Germans without coupons, and an occasional bit of butter or sausage when one of the women was sick.

They were in constant need of medicine, of sleeping pills, sedatives, and especially headache tablets and painkillers, since at any given moment some of them would be menstruating, and the doctors were not very cooperative. Here again Papa did his best for them.

Then he wangled a special authorization to take two of the women home for dinner once a week. Special authorizations of this kind were still obtainable at the time. The women had to be back in their barracks on Uhlandstrasse by ten o'clock. After a while he hit on the idea of bringing two women to Kaiserhofstrasse twice a week with the same authorization. On several occasions we entertained as many as six Russian women at a time. Sometimes I'd help him pick them up on Uhlandstrasse and bring them back.

It wasn't so easy deciding which of the women could be trusted not to tell anyone how he was abusing his special authorization. And there was no way to prevent the envy and possible suspicions of those who were not invited.

These evenings were always the same: dinner, conversation, exchange of political information, Papa's report on the situation at the fronts, especially the eastern front. He always told the truth, but the truth at that time could give our guests little hope of a speedy return home. That was in the winter of 1942–1943. True, the German Sixth Army had been surrounded and annihilated at Stalingrad, the German advance had been stopped, but the tide had not yet turned, and the end was not in sight.

After a while, when Papa felt surer of our guests, he took a still greater risk. After making sure that all the doors and windows were closed, he'd throw a woolen blanket over the radio to muffle the sound, and tune in Radio Moscow. Then all those present would put their heads under the blanket and listen to the latest news from the Soviet Union.

That was a dangerous ten or fifteen minutes. After the news bulletin Papa would switch off the radio, remove the blanket, and turn the dial to Radio Frankfurt, a vital precaution.

Those weekly gatherings worried me. It seemed unreasonable to take the risk of tuning in Moscow for these Russian women. I could see that they took very little interest in political or military news except when it affected them personally, when there was a report from their part of the country, for instance, or some word about the shipments of Russians or Ukrainians to Germany. It was the same when Mama tried to talk politics with them—they obviously didn't give a damn. Apart from their family worries, all they wanted to talk about was their own situation in Frankfurt and their work in the cogwheel factory. What really mattered to them was the bit of family life we gave them, the chance to be with people who showed them a little understanding and affection.

One day one of the Russian women became pregnant. She confided in Papa after missing her second period. In Fascist Germany, slave laborers were not allowed to bear children. The pregnancy would have to be terminated. Papa was not certain what the proper procedure was. He did not want the women in the barracks on Uhlandstrasse to get to work with knitting needles or other tools, so very reluctantly he reported the case to the personnel manager, who in turn notified the foreign workers' section of the Gestapo.

The next day two Gestapo agents came to the factory and questioned the woman. Papa was obliged to interpret. The agents tried to browbeat her into identifying the man, but got nothing out of her. She was taken to the hospital and given an abortion. She never came back to the factory word got out that she had been sent to a concentration camp near Darmstadt.

The personnel manager sent for my father and tried to justify himself for calling in the Gestapo. He wasn't an informer, he said, but he couldn't afford to stick his neck out. The Gestapo had given strict orders that all irregularities must be reported. After that, Gestapo agents came to the factory more and more often, and my father always had to interpret at their interrogations. When he came home, one look at him would tell us how bad they had been. Out of consideration for Mama's heart, he seldom went into detail. But now and then, when something was too hard for him to bear, he took me aside and told me about it. And sometimes he asked for my advice on one or another case.

In spite of the strict supervision, one or another of these Russian women kept getting pregnant. I know of two instances when Papa managed by a ruse to arrange for medical abortions without bringing the Gestapo into it. In accordance with his instructions, the women stayed in bed, complained of severe abdominal pain and profuse bleeding. This he reported to the personnel department. The next day he reported that the hemorrhage was no better and advised hospitalization. At the hospital a sympathetic gynecologist did the rest. On the third occurrence of such a hemorrhage, the management reported the case to the Gestapo, who demanded to see the medical record. This woman, like the first one, disappeared into a concentration camp.

For the first time Papa was suspected of making common cause with the Russian women and covering up their "offenses." The personnel manager threatened to report him to the Gestapo if it should be found that he neglected to report any irregularity connected with the Russian women.

Papa was terrified. Maybe it had never occurred to him that helping the Russian women could put him in such danger. He was a timid man, certainly no hero.

Back from the Dead

After that Papa was more careful. But his sympathy with the Russian women and their trust in him could not pass unnoticed. Too many eyes were watching him. And since he was too kindhearted for the work he was doing, the women often persuaded him to approve requests that had no chance of being granted and that only exasperated the management.

His superiors and fellow workers found fault with him for trying to make the Russian women's working and living conditions more humane. More and more often, he was accused of treating them with kid gloves and encouraging them to complain over every trifle. Friendly workers warned him, but apparently he didn't take their warnings seriously enough. One secretary in the personnel section even stopped him in the entrance and told him her office had been collecting evidence against him for some time.

In the end he was blamed for all the Russian women's misdeeds: going to the doctor too often, stealing, quarreling with German workers, poor work. But even then he couldn't bring himself to abandon them. He felt that they couldn't manage without him. He may have relied on his age to protect him.

He was all the more surprised when, on December 7, 1943, only a few days before his seventy-third birthday, the blow fell. At eight o'clock that morning, when as usual Papa arrived in Sachsenhausen with the Russian women, he was told that two Gestapo agents were waiting in the personnel department and that this time their business was not with the women but with him. There the agents informed him that he was under arrest and that they were taking him to headquarters on Lindenstrasse for questioning. They wouldn't let him go to his locker in the dressing room or communicate with anyone in the office or the machine shop. He asked if he could get in touch with his wife, but they said no, and even forbade the personnel director to notify us. One of the Gestapo agents would notify us in due time, they said.

Nevertheless, we got the news the same morning. Two hours later, a woman from the factory, probably the same secretary who had once warned Papa, rang our doorbell. My mother, who was alone at the time, opened the door. In the half-darkness of the stairwell the secretary told her what had happened and disappeared. She had taken a big risk, though she hardly knew Papa.

A car took him to Lindenstrasse. There he had to wait in a closed ground-floor room, with nothing in it but a table and a few chairs. He was all alone, his heart pounded, and he was in a cold sweat. He racked his brains: What could the Gestapo have against him? Nothing special had happened in the last few weeks at the factory or at the Russians' camp.

It didn't occur to him that some trifle might have tipped the scales, that a routine complaint might finally have led the management to report him to the Gestapo.

More than two hours later, he was led out for questioning. Three men were present, the two who had brought him from

Sachsenhausen and a third, apparently of higher rank, who sat at the desk and asked the questions. The two others stood at the window or sat on a sofa taking notes. They didn't say much.

My father was made to sit in the middle of the room, at some distance from the desk. The light from the window fell full on his face and he couldn't get a good look at his interrogator.

First my father had to state his name, place and date of birth, and so on. Then, the agents informed him that the barracks on Uhlandstrasse had been searched between eight and ten that morning. Among other items, reading matter had been seized—the interrogator brought his hand down on a small pile of books and magazines that lay on one corner of his desk—all in Cyrillic print. It would have to be checked out.

A sheet of paper with neat handwriting lay on the interrogator's desk. Looking down, he read a whole catalog of numbered charges, pausing after each item for emphasis. The document, he pointed out, had been submitted by the management of the firm. This, of course, came as no surprise to my father; no one else could have been familiar with so many details of what went on in the plant. And besides, it was common knowledge that the personnel department worked hand in glove with the Gestapo. It seemed that Papa was sabotaging the war effort. How? By encouraging the foreign workers to report sick and to complain about their allegedly bad working conditions; by covering up their offenses; by bringing the Russian women food or cast-off clothing from his home; by providing them with medicines, though he must have known this was expressly forbidden; by supplying them with books that had not previously been examined by the Gestapo; and lastly, by exceeding the provisions of his special permit authorizing him to take two Russian women home for dinner each week.

Next came a lecture. Was Herr Senger unaware that this was a fateful hour for the whole German nation, that war was everywhere, at the fronts and at home? Didn't he realize that all Russians were enemies, not only Russian soldiers, but civilians as well, and that included the Russian workers in Germany? Papa had expected a detailed interrogation; instead he was being treated to a lecture—a lecture full of veiled threats, to be sure. The interrogator must have thought he could break a feeble old man down and get him to talk by this sort of intimidation.

After this session, they took Papa down to the cellar and locked him up in a small barred cell. This cellar on Lindenstrasse had a ghoulish reputation. Any number of Communists, Socialists, and other "enemies of the state" had been tortured there and forced to give information about their illegal organizations; a good many had been killed. A young Communist, whom Papa had known personally, was believed to have hanged himself in one of these cells for fear of further tortures. Down there in the cellar Papa had time to think. He was most concerned about the accusations relating to the Russian women's barracks. He realized that one of the women must have denounced him, since they alone knew about the clothing, food, and medicine he supplied. And he knew at once who that woman must be; he had suspected her for quite a while.

She was in her middle thirties, the oldest of the lot. Unlike the other women, almost all of whom were of a rough peasant type, she was slender and delicate. She came from Sebastopol on the Crimean Peninsula and alone of all the women she could speak a few words of German. By way of explanation, she had told my father she had worked in a German officers' mess for a few months, where she had picked up her vocabulary. She was one of the first Papa had brought to our house. He was impressed by her city ways; she was better educated than the others, she had read quite a lot and seemed to take an interest in politics.

Sometime I'd notice that while she was chatting with Mama in Russian she would smile at me; and she showed her interest in other ways. One evening she came to our house with three other women. Right after dinner she said she wasn't feeling well and wanted to leave. She asked me if I'd mind taking her home. I didn't mind in the least, for I had an idea that something pleasant might come of it. I had guessed right. I knew no Russian, and with her smattering of German she couldn't say much, but it didn't take us long to get acquainted. In next to no time we were kissing and feeling each other up. But we didn't want to stop there, so we needed a secluded spot. I remembered a bench with elderberry bushes all around it on the Main embankment. Ionka and I had once spent a night on that bench, and from there it wasn't far to the barracks on Uhlandstrasse.

We were just settling down on the bench when suddenly we heard steps and voices nearby. We quickly disentangled ourselves and straightened our clothing. To our amazement we discovered that only ten or fifteen feet away, separated from us by a thick hedge, another couple had been making love. A police patrol had just caught them in the act.

While the police were busy checking their papers, I quietly fled, leading my companion by the hand. We ran through the bushes, circled the danger zone, passed the old municipal library, and returned to the river road.

An identity check would have been disastrous for both of us. But my companion seemed strangely unaware of the danger we'd been in. She was as cheerful and chatty as ever. Uhlandstrasse was pitch-dark in the blackout and she wanted to pull me into a doorway to carry on where we had left off. We still had more than half an hour's time. But for that night my enthusiasm was gone. She seemed so disappointed I tried to comfort her by promising to take her home again as soon as possible. I left her at the barracks gate, where she reported to the old night watchman.

As it happened, I never saw her again. Some of the other Russian women warned Papa. They were sure she hadn't been forced to come to Germany, she had come of her own free will to get away from her neighbors, who hated and despised her for hobnobbing with German officers in occupied Sebastopol.

Her forced transportation to Germany had really been flight from her own people. The women were also convinced that she spied on them. And as if that were not enough, an old mechanic under whom she worked passed on some of her confidences to Papa; it seemed that her husband was in a Soviet prison for political reasons, that her brother was fighting the Russians in Vlasov's army, and that she herself hoped the Germans would win the war.

After that Papa stopped taking her to Kaiserhofstrasse. It was lucky for us that she had been among the first to come, because that was before he had dared to tune in Radio Moscow when the women were there. And our dinner table conversation at the time was still noncommittal. At any rate, Papa didn't trust her any more and had stopped inviting her to our home. Apparently she had denounced him to get even.

He waited an hour in the barred cell. Then they came for him again. He knew the exact time, because they hadn't taken his watch or any of his belongings. They brought him something to drink and did not beat or torture him in any way. Such measures apparently were not considered necessary in the case of a seventy-three-year-old man. Probably in consideration of his age he was treated "correctly"—if such a word can be used in connection with the Gestapo.

It was then that the real interrogation began. The Gestapo officers shouted and threatened: he would be held until he confessed and denounced every one of his accomplices.

Then again he had to wait two hours in the barred cell. The third time the threats became louder and more violent. He'd better tell the truth and the whole truth or he'd end up in jail or even a concentration camp.

During a breathing spell, one of the agents pointed to the pile of books and asked which ones belonged to him. Papa showed him that there were three or four with his name written in Cyrillic script on the flyleaf. They were all Russian classics, he assured the agent, who leafed through them and let it go at that. Of course he didn't know a word of Russian.

After the third session my father was returned to the cellar. Someone even brought him a dish of thick soup but gave him no inkling of what was in store for him. He sat in his cell and waited. By then it was late afternoon.

In the meantime the following events had occurred at home. After hearing of Papa's arrest, Mama had asked a neighbor woman to phone Paula, Alex, and me, and tell us to come home. This was more complicated than it sounds, because no one in the whole back building had a phone; the nearest booth was on Fressgasse. Mama couldn't go herself, she hadn't the strength; by that time she spent most of the day in bed.

At noon we were all together, trying to decide what to do. We talked and talked, rejecting ideas as fast as we could think them up. We were very calm on the surface; I remember that. There was no sign of panic. Even Mama, whose fatal illness was already far advanced, remained cool.

We first decided to check the unknown woman's information, to find out if the Gestapo had really taken Papa away. I called up the factory and asked for Herr Senger. We could tell he'd been arrested by the hemming and hawing on the other end of the line. We packed a small suitcase with a few things we thought Papa would need, toilet articles, a shirt, a suit of underwear, a woolen sweater. We were sure that he must be either at the Gestapo or in one of the prisons, so at about two o'clock I phoned the Gestapo on Lindenstrasse and asked where we could take the suitcase.

Whoever answered said he could give us no information. Thereupon Paula took the suitcase to Lindenstrasse, which was about a fifteen-minute walk from Kaiserhofstrasse. She wasn't gone long. At the Gestapo they told her that if the person in question was being held there, we would find out soon enough.

By then it was late afternoon and we were really panicked. Alex was moaning and Paula was in tears. Mama lay in bed, her face as yellow as wax. On a chair beside her there was a basin of cold water—but Moissey wasn't there to make her cold compresses. From time to time she herself would dip a towel in the water, wring it out and lay it on her chest.

I had heard about the Gestapo's sadistic interrogation methods and horrible visions kept running through my head. I saw Papa being strapped to a chair, clubbed on the head, punched in the stomach, kicked; I saw him bleeding on the floor, whimpering and begging for mercy. There was no room in my head for any other images.

Mama closed her eyes, her pale lips moved; she seemed to be mumbling, though I couldn't hear a sound. Maybe she was talking to Papa, maybe she was saying a last goodbye to him.

Night fell, but we forgot to turn on the light; we sat in the dark waiting.

After an endless wait, Papa was brought up from the cellar. The Gestapo agent—the one who had begun the interrogation—told him they had decided to let him go. The decision had not been made lightly. Obviously he had been gravely at fault in his handling of the Russian women. Nevertheless, they were convinced that he was not an enemy of the people; he was merely too kindhearted, he had been led astray by false pity for the women entrusted to his care. He had failed to realize that in war one cannot be guided by the same feelings as in peace. "In your own interest," the interrogator concluded, "be more careful in the future, remember that a Russian is an enemy, and that enemies are not to be trusted."

Papa then had to sign a pledge to observe the strictest secrecy about his interrogation. Then he was let out. The Gestapo had held him for twelve hours.

It was about nine o'clock when we heard someone shuffling up the stairs. Could it be Papa? We held our breath and listened. It had to be Papa; we knew his heavy, weary step. That night it was heavier and wearier than usual.

The key turned in the lock, and Papa came in. He went slowly to Mama, bent over, and kissed her gently.

Than he kissed us children, one after another, as though counting to make sure we were all there. He picked up the enamel basin, put it on the dressing table, and sat down on the chair beside Mama's bed. He put his hands in his lap, let his head fall forward, and collapsed.

"O God!" Mama sighed—and as if that had been our cue, we all began to wail.

Papa had come back from the dead.

Bombs on Sachsenhausen

One midday in September 1944 there was a heavy air raid on Frankfurt. At the time I was working as section manager at the southern plant of Fries Jr. on Schulstrasse in Sachsenhausen. We were manufacturing essential military hardware, mostly torpedo racks for the navy and enormous buoys that looked like two cones placed tip to tip, which were used for marking minefields in the North Sea.

When the warning sounded, I was attending a conference at the main plant in Riederwald. I jumped on my bicycle and hurried to the nearest shelter. One could tell by the explosions and tremors that Frankfurt was once again the target. A voice on the radio told us that the planes were American and that they were dropping their bomb loads on Sachsenhausen.

When the all clear sounded, I cycled back to Sachsenhausen. Half an hour later I saw what the bombs had done. A "blockbuster," the blast of which is powerful enough to rupture the lungs of everyone within a radius of several hundred yards, had scored a direct hit on the factory's temporary shelter, which was used by the eighty-odd Russian forced laborers employed at the factory. For the Germans there was a solidly built bunker on Schifferstrasse, which was off limits to the foreign workers. The temporary shelter was protected by a layer of earth no more than two meters thick, which the smallest bomb would have penetrated. The place was so dangerous that no German was expected to set foot in it, not even the Russian women's supervisor. So during air raids the women were left without supervision, something that happened at no other time. I had seen how terrified they were in that shelter. They knew a direct hit would kill them all. At the sound of the first explosions nearby they would wail for their mamichkas; and some of them would pray.

When the bombs followed too soon after the warning and there wasn't enough time to reach the safe bunker on Schifferstrasse, a few Germans would slip into the temporary shelter. That's how it was this time. There were six Germans and seventy-eight Russian women in it when the blockbuster fell. All eighty-four were killed instantly. The only survivors among the Russian women were eight who, knowing there was no safety in the shelter, had hidden in the factory.

You could usually tell from the radio announcements whether or not the bomber formations were heading for Frankfurt. If they weren't, I would join the Russian women in the temporary shelter when the sirens blew. That morning it sounded as if the planes were headed somewhere else; if I hadn't been in Riederwald I'd have gone to the shelter because it was nearer. It was just a lucky break that that bomb didn't get me.

That very afternoon the bodies were taken away by a unit of the Technical Rescue Service. The entrance to the shelter had caved in, and it took several hours to get through, but then it was easy to reach the bodies. In every case death had been caused by ruptured lungs.

I stayed on at the factory in case my help should be needed for identification. The coffins didn't arrive until late in the day; in the meantime the dead Russian women and the Germans—two women, two children, a young antiaircraft auxiliary, and an elderly worker with a bad leg—lay side by side on brown wrapping paper. You'd have thought they were sleeping. A priest, who had been called in, said prayers and administered last rites. The families of the German victims arrived. Their wailing filled the yard.

No one mourned the dead Russian women.

There were air-raid warnings almost every night. The cellars of the wine shop in our front building had been converted into a shelter, and we spent many an hour there. It had steel doors, gas locks, air shafts, an emergency power unit, an infirmary, and other security installations, which however served more to lull the population than to provide real protection against bombs. When the sirens started howling during the night or, as was becoming more and more frequent, during the day, the inhabitants of all the houses in the vicinity ran to our shelter with their air-raid packs. There would be somewhere between eighty and a hundred people. Most of them were habitués and had their regular places. There they would sit trembling in anticipation of the horrible whistling sound that bombs make as they fall. That was Frau Morschhäuser's hour of glory. This resolute woman, the wife of the little lame tailor on the top floor, was our air-raid warden. She wielded sweeping authority during alerts, and she was a fanatical Nazi. In other words she was dangerous. All the tenants were afraid of her and took good care what they said in her presence. As badges of office, she wore a black-and-white armband with the letters LS* on it and a steel helmet that was supposed to shield her from shell fragments. She carried a first-aid kit slung over her shoulder, a flashlight fastened to her belt, and a "people's gas mask" in one hand.

She'd start commanding on the stairs. "Get a move on,

*LS, *Luftschutz*—Air Protection Service.

you. We all want to get there before the bombs start falling."
She and no one else told people where to sit, forbade them to
talk too loud or move around, scolded the children when they
began to get restless, decided when the iron door was to be
opened, threatened to report anyone who tried to go out for
three puffs during the alert, or to leave after the preliminary
all clear. She never sat down, she was always on the run,
keeping an eye on everything and everybody. And when she did
stand still for a moment, it was in the open gas door. That was
her command post.

Never before in her life had Frau Morschhäuser wielded
such authority, had so much power. In the air-raid shelter her
voice, her posture, her way of walking, everything about her
changed—to hear her comforting a frightened old woman, for
instance, you'd have thought she herself didn't know the meaning of fear.

Those hours when the bombs were turning the city into
rubble and ashes were the high points in Frau Morschhäuser's
existence. For once they made her feel alive, and for that I'm
sure she'd have liked the war and the air raids on Frankfurt to
go on forever. She knew the end of the war would mean the
end of her glory, and there'd be nothing to look forward to but
poverty and the hopeless obscurity of her husband's tailor shop.
Frau Morschhäuser, the tailor's wife, was one of those peculiar
growths, a kind of deadly nightshade, that flourished on the soil
of war and withered away when the war was over.

The following happened in January 1945. Mama had died
by then, Alex and I were in the army. As so often, Papa and
Paula were sitting in the air-raid shelter, in the places Frau
Morschhäuser had assigned them. Several waves of planes had
passed over. The cellar trembled as bombs fell nearby. Dust
flew from the cracks in the wall, making people cough. Children screamed, women moaned or wept or prayed. Papa and
Paula were as frightened as everyone else, because so many
bombs had never before been dropped on the inner city. Sud-

denly there was a terrible crash, the whole cellar was lifted up, bottles tumbled, there was a rattling of cups and saucers. The light went out. Screams. Then silence. Flashlights were lit. After a while the emergency generator started up, the bulbs glowed faintly. A dark cloud of dust hovered in midair, people choked and coughed and pressed damp cloths to their mouths and noses. From her command post in the gas door Frau Morschhäuser cried, "Attach gas masks. Keep them on until the dust settles." This was absurd; moist handkerchiefs had the same effect and were a lot more comfortable. But a few people obeyed. A few minutes later her drill sergeant's voice rang out again. "Keep calm, everybody. Our building is all right. A house in the neighborhood must have caved in."

The iron gas doors were flung open, the hum of the ventilators was heard, and little by little the dust was blown away. Everyone was relieved when Frau Morschhäuser announced that no one had been hurt or trapped beneath the rubble. The panic subsided.

Half an hour later the all clear sounded. The people all ran out into the street to see what had happened, but there was nothing to see. Everyone went home to get on with his interrupted sleep. Still somewhat dazed, Papa and Paula crossed the court to the back building. A few weeks before, the left half of the building had been hit by an incendiary bomb and had burned down. By that time only Papa and Paula were living in the right half, all the other tenants had been evacuated. Suddenly Papa stumbled and let out a cry; it was all Paula could do to hold him up. In the darkness he had almost fallen into a big hole that hadn't been there before. They looked into it with their flashlights but they couldn't see the bottom.

They guessed the hole had been made by some piece of wreckage from a shot-down bomber. When they looked out the window the next morning, they were horrified to see that the hole was almost exactly round and six or seven feet in diameter.

In the afternoon a bomb-disposal unit removed a thousand-pound bomb, the heaviest type used against Germany. It had fallen right next to our air-raid shelter and made a hole ten feet deep without exploding. If it had exploded, there wouldn't have been one survivor in the shelter, and nothing would have been left of 10, 12, or 14 Kaiserhofstrasse or their back buildings.

That bomb crater could be seen in the court until the 1960's, when No. 12 Kaiserhofstrasse was torn down to make way for a parking lot. It had been filled in with sand after the bomb was removed. The smaller children in the house used it as a sandbox; they played in it for years.

The Baker's Wife

One night in the spring of 1943 we had one of our worst air raids. When the all clear sounded, I left the shelter and ran up to the attic of the front building to look out and see where the bombs had struck and what was on fire.

I opened one of the skylights. It had to be lifted and fastened with a flat iron rod. That gave me a better view of the burning city. Just then a voice beside me asked, "Can I look too?"

It was the baker's young wife, who lived one floor below us in the back building, a luscious beauty with a pretty face and rather thick lips. She had more than her share of feminine curves, which she emphasized with tight-fitting sweaters and skirts. She had often smiled at me during our hours in the shelter, and then I'd have daydreams of lying in bed with her and feeling her skin next to mine.

"Sure, come on!" I let her step in front of me, because the space was too narrow for us to stand side by side.

The city was burning in many places. A large area was one

sea of flame. The fire had set up a wind that could be heard clearly from our window. The crackling of the flames mingled with the high-pitched bursts of ack-ack shells, which continued in spite of the all clear, as did the nervous play of the searchlight beams crossing the night sky in all directions.

"Good God!" cried the baker's wife when she saw all the flames, holding both hands up to her open mouth and leaning back a little. Our bodies touched.

"Look! Look over there!" she said, "do you see? That must be Sachsenhausen." She stuck her arm out the window and pointed south. I was surprised to hear her address me by the familiar *du*. She had never done that before. Maybe it was the excitement of the fire.

She bent her head to one side, so I could lean out to see Sachsenhausen. But heaven knows that at that moment, with my right cheek and right ear touching her hair, I couldn't tell one direction from another. All I could do was stammer, "Yes, that must be Sachsenhausen." I really couldn't tell if it was Sachsenhausen, Bornheim, or Seckbach, I didn't know and I didn't care. There were fires almost every night, but that hair! I pressed my chest against her shoulder as if to get a better view of Sachsenhausen, or of Seckbach, Bornheim, or whatever. She didn't move out of the way. Maybe I only imagined that her heart was thumping too.

Very gently, as though groping for something to hold on to, I touched her hip with my right hand. She was still looking straight ahead as though interested only in the blaze. "Oh, those flames!" she said. "Look! That must be Griesheim or Höchst! I wonder if they've hit the IG-Farben?"

"Could be," I said, breathlessly, meanwhile moving my hand forward along her hip and letting it rest on her belly, which I could feel rising and falling to the rhythm of her breathing.

It was a horrible, beautiful sight, on all sides big and little pillars of fire rising into the sky, and between them flat lakes of flame. From time to time, probably when a building collapsed, there would be a cascade of sparks, which might have been spewed out by some gigantic furnace.

"How awful! Look at that!" And she laid her hand on my exploring hand. Through her tight-fitting dress, I could feel the delightfully hilly region around her navel. She tapped my hand with one finger, her way of saying, "Keep it up, I like it." Thus encouraged, I pressed a little harder and she tapped again, meaning, "Go on, that's fine." In the end I was holding her so tight that my arm ached.

At that point the baker's wife had to lean farther forward; she must have discovered a new blaze in the inner city or something else demanding her concentrated attention. In any case she shifted her weight, and I had to join in her movement, for I still had my hand on her belly. What a firm, sturdy ass she had! And that precipitous cleft, which divided the splendor in two. The play of her muscles brought out every detail. And meanwhile she went on talking about Sachsenhausen and Bornheim and all the other neighborhoods where fires were raging, but more softly now, and a hoarseness had come into her voice.

Since the skylight narrowed her field of vision and she wanted to see everything, she had to twist her torso to the left and right. And since her ass joined in the movement and she often changed directions, while I stood glued to the spot, the friction was considerable and made for considerable warmth.

Quite of its own accord, my hand, which had been lying flat on her navel, slid downward to her crotch. I felt the seam of her panties and my nervous fingers took it as a welcome guide.

"I like you," I whispered in her ear.

"Hey!" she said. "You're breathing so hard."

"No one's to blame but you," I whispered hoarsely.

For the first time she turned her head toward me and smiled. As the fire raged outside and the ack-ack shells went on bursting, my fingers bravely climbed her most secret hill. Again she laid her hand on mine, but not invitingly, this time it was to hold me back. "Stop!" she said. "Somebody might see us."

Indeed, other tenants had meanwhile stationed themselves at other skylights, in every case two to a skylight, to look at the fires. Of course they couldn't see what we were doing, it was much too dark, but if the baker's wife was anxious, what could I do? My hand retreated to her belly, and I contented myself with tracing the circumference of her navel with one finger. That too was very pleasant. We stood there for quite a while, breathing hard. Then she detached her ass and back from me, turned around, and said softly, "Come down after a while. I'll be waiting for you." And she vanished in the darkness of the stairwell.

I stood there at the skylight in a daze, staring at the pillars and pools of fire. When everyone else had gone, I was still standing there, smelling her hair and the faint odor of sweat on the back of her neck, and feeling each one of our points of contact as though she were still standing there. Slowly I went down the stairs, across the court, and up to my room. Mama and Papa were already back in bed, Paula was busy in the kitchen. I lay down on my bed with my clothes on. What a rare opportunity was offered me, the kind of thing I had hardly dared hope for. All I had to do was get up, go downstairs, and knock on the door, and, with a soft creaking, paradise would open up to me.

Yet I hesitated. Eighteen steps down a woman was waiting for me, and I lay motionless on my bed, weighing the pros and cons, but knowing all the while that my weighing would come to nothing. I lay on my bed and let the baker's wife wait.

The baker and his wife had moved into our back building only two years before. He was in the SA, and before going off to the army six months earlier, he had often shown himself in his SA uniform. She belonged to the League of National Socialist Women and wore a big Nazi brooch on her coat. In the air-raid shelter she encouraged the terrified tenants with stiff-upper-lip, do-or-die slogans that she'd brought back from her Nazi meetings.

In the next few days I did my best to avoid her. But I couldn't help running into her now and then. Except for the coldest sort of greeting, she didn't say a word. Only once, passing me on the stairs, she hissed, "Yellowbelly!"

In the weeks that followed, I couldn't help noticing with a dumb, unreasonable jealousy that despite the wartime shortage of men the baker's wife had no need of me. She had other strings to her bow. But that didn't stop her from greeting all and sundry with a brisk "Heil Hitler!" or from babbling her do-or-die slogans in the air-raid shelter as the bombs rained down. In love and war, she remained a zealous Nazi, faithful to her Führer.

Mama's Last Journey

Her life was hard and so was her death. Until her sick heart finally stopped beating in the fall of 1944, it had struggled painfully on for months and years, flickering like a spent candle. By then we were living with Mimi in Jügesheim. Mama never gave up, she was determined to see the day when she'd be able to cry out, "We've made it. Now we don't have to be afraid any more."

Which of us knew what it was to be unafraid? We children had never known what it felt like to be free from fear. Mama and Papa had forgotten—but how we looked forward to that experience! After all the fear she had lived through, Mama certainly deserved to live at least that long, and she'd have made it if there had been a spark of justice up there where the question of life or death is supposedly decided.

When Mama was alive, I had never dared to tell her how much I loved her. Now that she was dead, I made up for lost time. At last I could give her all my love, and she had time to receive it. I took her head in my hands, stroked the wisps of gray hair out of her face, closed her eyes, and kissed her for the first time. Papa was in despair. The tears ran down his face. "What's to become of us now?" he moaned, and flung himself on the body. The rest of us tiptoed into the other room, leaving him alone with his grief.

I took it into my head that Mama shouldn't be buried in Jügesheim but in Frankfurt. Not in the Jewish cemetery, of course, that was impossible. But this was late 1944 and even in a Christian cemetery it wouldn't be so simple. I phoned the Frankfurt Cemeteries Bureau and was told that they were no longer able to arrange proper funerals for all the people who died a natural death or were killed in Allied air raids in Frankfurt and it was therefore impossible to accept deceased from outside the city. All the outlying townships had received strict instructions to authorize no transfers.

I shall never know why it was this particular issue, which was of no importance whatever to any of us—what, after all, did it matter whether Mama was laid to rest in a non-Jewish cemetery in Jügesheim or in Frankfurt?—that fanned the spark of rebellion in me. At any rate, I decided that with or without a permit, Mama was going to be buried in Frankfurt.

I knew it was foolish, I knew it was dangerous, but I couldn't help it. For the first time a decision was up to me. Mama had always held the reins of the family chariot, and now they had automatically fallen to me. So at the very first opportunity I made a decision that Mama would certainly not have made. I didn't ask for anyone else's opinion. Mama was going to be buried in Frankfurt, and that was that.

In October 1944, when American and British planes were dropping bombs on German towns and villages day and night, it was not easy to find someone willing to transport a dead body to Frankfurt. The trip from Jügesheim via Offenbach to Frankfurt would take a horse-drawn vehicle a good three hours. Actually, considering that driver and wagon would have to come back to Jügesheim, it would take six hours, not counting the time spent in Frankfurt and the almost inevitable delays caused by air-raid alarms. And a motor vehicle was out of the question, since in that phase of the war neither gasoline nor cars were available for private purposes. I soon realized that if anyone could help me it was Franz Winter, the village carpenter and undertaker, who was the proud owner of a gleaming ebony hearse with crossed silver palm fronds on the sides and back. He kept it in a shed behind the mortuary.

When he and his assistant came to take Mama away, they had to leave the coffin in the entrance and carry the body, wrapped in a sheet, down the narrow stairs. They had to bend it at a sharp angle, and a ghastly sound—something like a deep sigh—came out of Mama's mouth. As Franz Winter screwed the lid on the coffin, I asked him if he would be willing—for good money, of course—to take the body to Frankfurt.

The mere idea put him in a rage. All the way to Frankfurt? Why not America? What with the bombers coming and going! I came from Frankfurt myself; didn't I know what was going on there and in Offenbach, not to mention the East Port, which we'd have to pass through. It was just too dangerous, he said, he wouldn't do it for any amount of money; why did I have to bury my mother in Frankfurt, I should get the whole idea out of my head, she'd be just as well off in Jügesheim.

But by then I had come to regard my project as a test of character, and I simply couldn't give in. That night I went to see the carpenter. In my pocket I had a bottle of schnapps that I had been saving a long time for some very special occasion.

I pleaded with him; I told him it had been Mama's last wish to be buried in Frankfurt. This out-and-out lie, the schnapps, and a hundred-mark note turned the trick when I'd almost given up hoping. The carpenter agreed to take Mama to the Frankfurt Central Cemetery in his hearse. He didn't even ask me if I had the required papers. He took that for granted.

We started off on the morning of October 24. It was a cold rainy day. I sat beside the carpenter in the driver's seat.

186 | Mama's Last Journey

He wasn't very talkative. I had the feeling that Mama's eyes
were on me and that made me uneasy because I knew she
wouldn't have approved of this trip. I kept turning round,
thinking she might have something to say to me. On top of
everything else, I was frozen through.

*

I know, Mama, I know you'd have battered the coffin lid
with your fists if you had known what this trip cost and known
that I had no permit. *"Meshugge!"* you'd have said. *"Meshugge* the whole lot of you. Throwing all that money out of
the window. For what? For a *goyim naches.* * What are you
trying to do? Get yourself a place in heaven by taking my dead
body for a ride? Without a permit yet? You think you're a hero,
maybe?" And she'd certainly have wound up with her eternal
refrain: "As if we haven't got *tsuris* enough already!"

And again, as so often in the past, you'd have been right,
Mama. I had a guilty conscience. When I think it over, I
realize that I always had a guilty conscience when I was with
you. But why?

I won't start arguing with you now about the mistakes I
may have made or what I did right. The present occasion, this
trip to Frankfurt in the hearse, is much too sad for that. But,
Mama, could you tell me this at least: Why were you always
drumming it into me to be careful, to hide, to make myself
inconspicuous, always to take a back seat, to apologize, to
cringe, and keep quiet? Because that's what gave me a guilty
conscience day and night.

You brought us up to be servile. All right, all right. You'll
clench your fists and cry out to high heaven: "It's the price of
survival, Valya! The price of survival!" That may be. But I
can't help blaming you all the same. If only once you had told
me to hit back!

You were a typical Jewish *mameh.* You'd have let yourself

Goyim naches—Foolishness suitable only for non-Jews.

be torn to pieces for your family. But something was wrong. Could it be that you tried to transplant your south Russian world to Kaiserhofstrasse?

You taught us to swim in a sea of lies and turned lying into a vital element. Of course a thousand accidents and a few miracles helped, but without the lies the miracles wouldn't have been enough to save our lives. But what a life!

*

The road to Offenbach dragged on endlessly. The drizzle kept on and on. The carpenter buried his head deeper and deeper in his turned-up coat collar and cursed the weather, the horses, and his load. At first he exchanged a few words with me, but then, when he wasn't cursing, he would talk only to his two bony nags; and they'd nod their heads, as if to say that they understood his complaints and agreed with him. From time to time he would bring his whip down wearily on the black oil-cloth cover he had thrown over the horses when the rain got worse. The sound would frighten the horses and they'd quicken their pace for a while, but then they'd fall back into their usual slow trot.

At a certain point the carpenter stopped talking to me altogether; he seemed angry. I didn't know why, unless he was regretting that he had agreed to make the trip or unless he blamed me for the bad weather.

Let him be angry, then he wouldn't disturb my silent dialogue with Mama; then I could busy myself with my thoughts.

I was feeling really low. I'd have liked to cry, it might have made it all easier. But in those hours on the road to Frankfurt with my dead mama behind me, I couldn't. I just felt a horrible weight on my chest.

During the first part of the trip I was upset by the way the coffin creaked as we jolted over the bumpy road. I felt like plucking the carpenter's sleeve and saying, "Couldn't you drive more carefully, my mama's in there." But after an hour and a half I hardly cared what went on around me. The coffin was far from my thoughts. At times I even forgot to think about my dead Mama.

I was tired. My one wish was to creep away and lie down somewhere, to sleep and forget.

Under the rain the dingy gray house fronts of bomb-shattered Offenbach looked even more desolate than usual. They answered my own mood exactly. The city was in deep mourning. But the color of its mourning wasn't black like that of our hearse, which glistened almost provocatively in the rain; it was gray, dusty gray; and that was the color of the sky and of the Main and of the few people who crossed our path. An old woman stopped on the sidewalk and quickly crossed herself. I imagine she always crossed herself at the sight of a hearse, just as in childhood we'd spit on our left thumb and screw it into our right palm when we saw a white horse, that brought good luck, or fart when we saw a mounted policeman, and even if it was only the tiniest little fart we could be sure nothing bad would happen to us for the rest of the day.

We passed through Offenbach without difficulty. Then we had to take the Fechenheim Bridge across the Main. We were right in the middle of the bridge when the air-raid warning sounded. We had a few minutes' time even so, because it was only a pre-alert.

"Should we go back?" the frightened carpenter asked.

"No, forward," I said. "It's no farther to the Fechenheim bunker than back to Offenbach." At that, he lashed the flanks of the horses, right and left, and shouted "Gee-up." Reluctantly the weary horses speeded up a little. The coffin rumbled more loudly, and I remembered Mama again, poor Mama, whose last excursion was to end so dismally.

By the time we reached the bunker, the all clear sounded. We stopped all the same, and the carpenter watered his horses. Then we went on. A little later we came to a busy intersection on the main artery leading eastward out of Frankfurt. I had hoped to avoid the place, where there were constant police checks, but bomb craters and the wreckage of bombed buildings had made the parallel road impassable.

So we were forced to pass through Mainkur, as that intersection was called. My heart pounded when, still some distance away, I saw the red signal disks of the military police who were stopping and inspecting all vehicles. I hadn't let on to the carpenter that I had no permit. I hadn't even confided my worry about this checkpoint. We were stopped by two M.P.'s. We handed them our passports and the death certificate the doctor had made out. They studied my stateless passport at great length—I was used to that; one of them leafed through it, looked at the photograph, then at me, then returned the passport. I could tell by the look on his face that he wasn't entirely happy about it. The carpenter had to get out and open the hearse to prove we were not trying to smuggle black-market goods or living persons into the city. They had no objection to our transporting a dead body; either they were unfamiliar with the regulations or they took the death certificate for a transfer permit. One of them, while folding up the death certificate, asked me on a note of sympathy if the dead woman was my mother, and which cemetery we were headed for. When I spoke of the Central Cemetery, which was nearest, he seemed to approve. Then they let us drive on. After that we were in the city proper, where no one would think of checking up on a hearse. The rain had stopped, so my dead mama's entry into Frankfurt was a little more cheerful than the ride from Jügesheim.

For half an hour we rolled over the cobblestones of Hanauer Landstrasse. It was rough going. The horses' hooves clattered on the cobbles, the hearse was shaken so hard that it groaned, and in spite of the blanket spread out on the seat, my bottom felt bruised and battered.

We were in the midst of a traffic snarl in one of the narrow streets of Bornheim when the sirens blew. We drove to the nearest public shelter, the carpenter hitched the horses to a lamppost, and down we went.

The shelter was a damp cellar. Most of the people there were elderly and scared out of their wits. As we sat wedged in among them, I wondered what would happen if a bomb fell nearby—which was perfectly possible—and the horses broke loose. I had visions of the two terrified horses galloping driverless through the streets of Bornheim with my dead mama; I saw the hearse turning over as it raced around a curve. From minute to minute I grew more nervous.

I remember that shelter well, because suddenly a woman ran in screaming. What was the trouble? The trouble was a hearse right outside the shelter and she wanted to know if the driver was present. When the Jügesheim carpenter spoke up, she showered him with reproaches. Couldn't he have parked his hearse a hundred yards down the street? Did he want to attract death to the house? Of course he had no such intent. No one in the cellar said a word. Evidently those people saw nothing unreasonable in the woman's fears, and I'm sure most of them felt the same way: If only the fellow had parked his hearse somewhere else!

We were in luck. No bombs fell on Bornheim that morning. Half an hour later the all clear sounded.

Since we were already approaching the cemetery, I could no longer put off telling the carpenter that I had neither a transfer permit nor an authorization to bury my mother in this or any other Frankfurt cemetery. I had to tell him before we got there, because under certain circumstances the plan I had worked out would require his cooperation.

His reaction was worse than I had feared. He was beside himself. He wanted to turn round and drive straight back to Jügesheim. He pulled up at the curb and reined in his horses. I tried in vain to mollify him. Passersby were beginning to stare at us. It was very embarrassing.

The carpenter's agitation was typical of the times. He was terrified at the thought of having—even unsuspectingly and against his will—infringed on any regulations. After ten years of Fascism the most pronounced characteristic of the German people was fear of the party and of the government. The slightest misdemeanors were punished as major crimes. And the people reacted accordingly. Their attitude toward one another and toward the authorities was dominated by fear.

I, too, lived in fear for many years, and so did my family —and the average German's fear was hardly comparable to our constant fear of being discovered. Nevertheless, or perhaps in a way for that very reason, I tried later on to summon up a little understanding for their fears.

The terrified carpenter wanted absolutely no truck with the police. His worst fear was that his hearse might be confiscated. Nothing I could say made any impression. He finally calmed down, but only because he realized that he couldn't very well drive the body back to Jügesheim. And then he asked me what I was planning to do.

Some fifty yards in front of the main entrance to the cemetery there was a somewhat smaller gate; that was the one the hearses always used. I had noticed that it was never closed during the day, and that no one checked the vehicles going in. I was pretty sure burial permits were checked only on the platform of the mortuary behind it, where the coffins were unloaded.

My plan was to drive right in and pull up at the mortuary. The carpenter and I would unload the coffin. If we were asked for papers I'd stall for time until Franz Winter had driven his hearse away. I told him to beat it as soon as the coffin was unloaded. What could the cemetery people do but keep it? They couldn't put an occupied coffin out in the street, could they? They'd rant and rave awhile, and then they'd agree to bury my mother and even assign us a plot. If the worst came to the worst, I'd have to pay a fine.

So we drove in. At the mortuary, we jumped down off the seat and pulled out the coffin—all the while I was begging

Mama's forgiveness for being in such a hurry to leave her. A workman, who was standing there in a greenish-gray work smock, helped us to lift the coffin on to a trolley.

A guardian appeared and asked for the burial papers. As slowly as possible I produced the death certificate and held it out to him. Still in a friendly tone, he asked me for the other papers. I pretended not to understand. Losing his patience, he asked again for the other papers, and I told him the truth, that I didn't have any, not even a municipal certificate.

Meanwhile, the carpenter had climbed back on his seat. He was just getting ready to drive away, when apparently the guardian caught on to my trick. He turned around, and in a very different voice ordered the carpenter to stay right where he was until the matter of the papers was settled.

Franz Winter had been much too slow. He should have been gone by then. And now he was stuck. This was a possibility that hadn't occurred to me.

The guardian turned back to me. He was furious. He was strictly forbidden, he shouted, to accept bodies for burial without proper papers and previous arrangements. We'd just have to take the body away again. I couldn't blame him, he was only doing his job. But I argued all the same. I said I wouldn't dream of taking the body away, as citizens of Frankfurt we had a perfect right to bury our dead in a Frankfurt cemetery. And then I told him a big lie, that the Cemeteries Bureau had told me on the phone to bring in the body even without conveyance papers and assured me that arrangements would somehow be made for burial in the Central Cemetery.

The guardian wouldn't buy it. The Cemeteries Bureau should have known better, regulations were regulations, and that was that. I'm sure he'd never been in such a situation before, and he got more and more excited. But what was he to do? In theory, such a thing couldn't happen. But in practice, a dark-brown coffin with my mother in it was there on the trolley. For the tenth time the guardian looked at the death certificate. Then he said that whoever this deceased might be he couldn't accept her without the approval of the administration. I saw there was nothing for it and suggested that we go together to the administration building which was across the way and straighten things out. At least I'd be gaining a little time.

I looked at the carpenter in his driver's seat. I was curious to see how he was taking all this. To my surprise, he grinned at me and winked, as if to let me know that he'd do his part toward bringing our business to a successful conclusion. He hadn't been so lively and cheerful all morning. I must say that I didn't understand him, but I forgave him for his sulking between Jügesheim and Offenbach. I'd have gladly promised to get him a seat in heaven if everything came out all right.

At the administration office everything went off smoothly. As was to be expected, the superintendent gave me another bawling out. With a war going on, you don't go carting dead bodies around the country without a permit; the regulations were perfectly clear. Where would we be if everybody started doing just as he pleased?

But I could tell by his tone that his harsh words were for the guardian's benefit. After saying his piece he sent the guardian away, told me to sit down, and asked me exactly what I wanted. I don't remember the rest of our conversation, but the upshot was that I got my authorization. Though the crematorium was being kept very busy at the time, arrangements were made for cremation and urn burial, which is what I'd wanted all along.

This superintendent had wished from the start to be helpful. Luckily, when my family moved out to Jügesheim, we had neglected to register our departure from Frankfurt with the police. Consequently we were still residents of Frankfurt officially, as he confirmed by a phone call, and that gave the proceedings a relatively legal look.

Even so, such kindness on the part of an official during the Hitler period was most unusual. Without it, coffin and body might ultimately have remained in Frankfurt, but I'd have had to spend whole days running from office to office and probably have had to pay a heavy fine.

Meanwhile Franz Winter, the village carpenter and undertaker, had been doing just what I had wanted him to do in the first place. The moment we disappeared into the administration building, he had given his horses a flick of the whip and driven his hearse through the open gate. As far as Mainkur, as he told me some days later, he had urged his horses on, but once he was sure no one was following he had slowed down. Right after Offenbach, realizing that the excitement had made him thirsty, he had stopped for a beer and stayed for another. It was late in the day before he got back home to Jügesheim and unharnessed his horses.

My Heart Defect

Early in the summer of 1944 I had received my draft notice, and Alex had got his a week later. This mass levy was known as the "Goebbels call-up" and included all foreigners living in Germany, insofar as they were not being held in internment camps.

I had talked it over with Alex. We tried to figure out some way of evading the call. We didn't see how the doctor at the induction center, who examined dozens of recruits every day for possible venereal diseases, could possibly fail to notice a ritually circumcised penis.

But what could we do? Fail to show up? They'd come and get us. Disappear? But where to? Even if it were possible, our disappearance would lead the authorities to our parents, and that would inevitably be the end of them. We'd just have to report; we had no choice.

I had seldom been so frightened. For several nights before we had to go, I kept having the same horrible nightmares. Four men, army doctors no doubt, would be holding me by the arms and legs, trying to pull me apart. I'd wake up screaming and do my best to stay awake for fear they'd start torturing me again if I fell asleep.

Mama had been totally composed when I said goodbye to her on the morning of the fateful day. She had only said, "Come back in good health, Valya." Papa took me to the door and kissed me on both cheeks. I can still feel his stubbly beard on my face. His voice trembled as he whispered, "Dear Valichka," and the tears ran down over his gray beard. He held my head in both hands and looked at me as if he had something to say; then he let me go, but forgot to lower his hands, and for a while they hovered in midair.

By then Papa had sunk into a state of apathy and resignation. He didn't give us one word of encouragement; no ideas, no suggestions. Paralyzed by fear, he took things as they came, with an infinite Jewish sadness. But was my own behavior any different? What risks was I taking?

So I went to the induction center on Wiesenhüttenstrasse; I was burning up with fear, but I went. I dragged my feet as if my shoes had been made of lead, every step was torture. I was pursued by visions of the doctor examining me, unmasking me as a Jew; I saw myself arrested and instantly sent to the gas chambers, without even a chance to notify Mama and Papa.

Then I was standing before the sergeant, and there was no more time for visions. Present draft notice, fill out blank, wait, undress except for shorts, wait some more, file into the examining room with eight or ten others, all in alphabetical order.

Then came the moment I had been dreading for the last ten days: "Pants off" and "Place pants on table." The orders were given by a medical sergeant who stood to one side. The doctor passed along the line, inspecting the private parts of the "Goebbels call-up" as meticulously as if victory or defeat depended on it.

Trembling, I looked on as the men ahead of me were examined. The penis was first examined in a hanging position, then the recruit had to lift it to show the underside; in some cases the doctor felt the scrotum. Then the recruit had to pull back his foreskin. It all went very quickly, each new recruit copied the movements of the man ahead of him.

While the doctor was examining the others, I had ample opportunity to compare myself with them and note the difference. It was unmistakable. Me with my smoothly rounded glans, the others with their tapering foreskins. Their penises didn't all look alike; some were shriveled, one looked like a bald head swathed in a muffler, one looked like the tip of a carrot. But none was anything like mine.

Then it was my turn. First inspection in the hanging position. For a moment, I think, my heart stood still. I watched the doctor's face for the look of surprise that would greet my circumcised penis. I detected no expression, not a quiver, not a movement. Could it be that he really didn't notice? Lift penis, pull back foreskin—in a manner of speaking. That was it. Showing no sign of surprise, no interest, no expression whatsoever, the doctor moved on to the next in line.

The examination was over, we were told to dress. I still couldn't understand why the army doctor hadn't said anything; I mulled it over all the way home. Could it be that his indifference was put on, that he had noticed the absence of that fragment of foreskin which distinguishes a Gentile from a Jew?

A week later Alex was examined at the same induction center, possibly by the same doctor. He wasn't asked to account for his circumcision any more than I was.

In September 1944 my brother Alex was shipped to an armored infantry camp in Kassel, and a month later, a few days after Mama's death, I was sent to an artillery training camp in Fritzlar. Leaving Papa and Paula at home with their grief, their worries, their *tsuris,* I dutifully went off to the assembly point.

I still remember four of the recruits in my barracks. One was an eighteen-year-old volunteer from a village near Duderstadt, the son of a veterinarian; he was in such a hurry to become a soldier that he left secondary school in the middle of his last year, and four months after induction he was reported missing on the eastern front. The second was a musician from Göttingen, who lamented from morning to night about his bruised and battered hands, which may have been adept enough at the cello, but were all thumbs with a rifle and worse with a 150-mm. field howitzer; the third was the son of Friedrich Bethge, the writer and glorifier of Hitler; he never wearied of singing his father's praises, and never stopped talking about the racial elite, the spirit of ancient Greece, and the dignity of man; and the fourth was a public prosecutor at the Court of Exception in Kassel, with a little birdlike face and a high piping voice that gave me the creeps.

In the evening the prosecutor liked to talk about his work. His court had jurisdiction over "crimes against the German people": looting, inciting to rebellion, racial offenses, and so on. He'd tell us how hard it was to make himself understood by the foreign workers he had to prosecute and about the death sentences he had demanded and obtained. Then he'd describe in chilling detail a guillotining he'd witnessed.

Once he told us how a man who had just moved to Kassel had been arrested on the strength of a denunciation. It turned out that his papers were forged. The Gestapo handed him over to the judicial authorities. The prosecutor had gone to a good deal of trouble and finally, after a long and complicated investigation and interrogation, unmasked the man as a Jew. And on a note of regret he concluded: "When the Jew saw there was no possible way out, he hanged himself in his cell before we could even try him." In short, the prosecutor noted, the Jew had sentenced himself.

It might, I reflected, have been my brother Alex or I who had fallen into the clutches of this bird-faced public prosecutor. Once again I had a vision of myself hanging, this time not head down by the bars of the stairwell window, but feet down with my head on a slant. And I could hear the prosecutor announcing in his piping voice, "He sentenced himself." I couldn't see Alex hanging himself, I knew he'd have fought to his last breath.

The climax of our training was a stay of several weeks at a "hardening camp" on a hilltop near Fritzlar. The nights were bitter cold. The mercury fell to well below freezing. I came down with a sore throat and a high fever. The doctor diagnosed diphtheria and ordered me to report to the military hospital. That was in mid-January 1945. I packed my few personal belongings in a carton and reported to the nearby Ursuline convent, which had been turned into a reserve hospital.

Naturally I was put in the contagious ward. Fine, they wouldn't be able to send me to the front for quite some time. Before they could take me off the contagious list they'd have to send three smears to Kassel for analysis, and that would take at least three weeks. The first two smears were negative, but the third was positive, which meant, though my sore throat had cleared up long ago, that I was still contagious and would have to remain in the hospital.

But after a month I was ready to be discharged. A medical sergeant brought me the news; my unit was leaving for the eastern front, and I was to report back to the army post within forty-eight hours.

But that same day a hospital train arrived from the eastern front, and a new patient was brought into our ward. He was shaking with fever, his whole body was covered with red blotches, and he had a blinding headache. A few hours before I was supposed to leave, the doctor diagnosed spotted typhus. Our ward, which had ten soldiers in it at the time, was put under absolute quarantine, and once again my discharge was postponed. The doctor said we'd be quarantined for at least four weeks. My battery went to the eastern front without me and, as I later found out, suffered heavy losses almost immediately.

The typhus patient, to whom we were indebted for our quarantine, was sent to Bad Wildungen for special treatment, but too late; he died a few days later.

Just before I was quarantined, Alex came to see me in the hospital. He was on his way back to Kassel after a short home leave; his unit would soon be leaving for the eastern front. He made quite a detour to come to Fritzlar and he brought me a cake from Mimi. Before parting, we promised each other to desert to the enemy at the first opportunity. Of course we were kidding ourselves; we both knew that in the final phase of the war both sides had stopped taking prisoners, that by this time there was only universal slaughter.

I said goodbye to Alex at the hospital gate and looked after him until he disappeared in the darkness. My heart grew heavy. I loved my brother Alex more than anyone in the world, and something told me I'd never see him again.

To this day I feel partly to blame for my brother's death. In sleepless nights I think of what I might have done to save him. I was older, more experienced; I should have done something—anything!—to stop him from going to the front. Why didn't I hit him, break a bone or two, send him to the hospital? But I let him go, I never tried to stop him. Alex trusted me. If I had implored him to hide, maybe in some corner of Frankfurt, he'd have taken my advice, he'd have had a chance of survival. I knew his chances of survival on the eastern front were negligible. But I didn't say a word.

Alex, who was always cheerful, who never doubted that he would live to see the end of the Third Reich, who on his way to the front continued to write letters full of optimism, who in the inferno of the front lines went on making plans for the future and writing them down and sending them home by army post, my brother, Alex, then barely twenty, was killed in one of the very last battles of the war by those with whom he sided and in whom he had placed all his hopes of a better future.

I've never been able to figure out why, but the doctor in charge of our ward, a Viennese, I don't remember his name, took a strange, somewhat mysterious liking to me. When I came down with a light case of typhus some days later, he sat on my bed and said to me so softly that no one else could hear, "You're not going to conk out so soon before the end! The war will be over soon. When that happens you've got to be on your feet. So pull yourself together."

And another time, when I was already better: "Have you ever stopped to think of your situation in this hospital? Either you'll be sent to the front with the next shipment, or the Americans will nab you."

"I know, but what can I do about it?"

"You'll have to figure that out for yourself. God helps those who help themselves." And after a pause he went on, "I've been thinking about it myself. The best would be to get hold of some civilian clothes and slip away to the country. Find some farmer to stay with. That would probably be the safest."

He examined me without a word, pulled up my blanket, bent over me, and whispered, "Want me to tell you what to do? Beat it, friend. Beat it on the double!" And he turned to the next patient.

These conversations, though in whispers, were possible only because the room was rather a large one and, once my typhus was diagnosed, my bed had been moved a little distance away from the others, so that he could be sure of not being overheard. I could see very clearly that he never spoke so long to anyone else in the ward. But I had no opportunity to take his advice. Two days later American artillery fire could be heard. To judge by the news bulletins that came in over the radio, Allied armored columns were advancing almost without opposition.

The hospital was in a turmoil. The nuns scurried along the corridors looking like frightened moths in their ankle-length black-and-white habits. Novices, lay nurses, doctors, and medical noncoms were running in all directions. The sirens sounded the alarm several times a day. Then we'd have to pick up our gas masks and file down the stairs to the cold, cramped cellars of the convent; we ten patients from the quarantined ward always went last; they put us in a tiny little room, where we were packed as tightly as the cockroaches that crowded into the corners at our approach.

A lay nurse I'd made friends with during the long quarantine offered to put me up at her home should the hospital be decommissioned. Her place was right near the convent and she told me how to get there without being noticed. She said it was better to be taken prisoner than to be shipped to the front, and she was certainly right. Once the hospital was abandoned, it wouldn't be more than two or three days before the Americans arrived and then I'd be saved. I was afraid, I hesitated, and let the opportunity go by.

Our quarantine had long since been lifted. All ambulant patients were ordered to put on their uniforms and report to the artillery post. Thus many of those who had hoped confidently to stay in the hospital until the end of the war were shipped to the front and, as likely as not, to their deaths.

To make sure that none of the sick soldiers took the wrong direction on their way to the barracks, a number of noncoms from the artillery training battalion had come to the hospital to escort them.

I was sitting on my bed in my uniform and boots, waiting for my marching orders and chain-smoking cigarettes I had rolled myself. Generous tobacco rations had been distributed on the last day: three packages to a man, after we had gone without for weeks. There was no cigarette paper, but we had learned to make do with newspaper.

From time to time a sergeant appeared in the doorway, called out a name or two, and handed the man his hospital discharge papers. A last handshake, and one after another marched off to the army post. I never saw any of them again.

There were only two of us left, a young steelworker from Soest, and myself. The worker's left arm had been amputated and he was shaking with wound fever. The man had lost his will to live and the doctor knew he couldn't help him. It was just two weeks since his mother and fifteen-year-old sister had been killed in an air raid on Dortmund. He had wept for days and after that he had hardly said a word to anyone, just lain there with his eyes closed.

I sat beside him and tried to give him courage. "Try and bear up," I said. "At least the war is over as far as you're concerned." What else could I say? I laid my hand on his burning head; for a moment he opened his eyes and looked at me. "Good luck," he said in a whisper. "I hope you get home all right." His right hand touched mine. I could have cried.

The sergeant came in again. It had to be my turn, but there were no papers in his hand.

"Recruit Senger."

I stood up and gave him a questioning look.

"Report at once to the hospital commander. Is that understood?"

"Yes, sir."

I didn't get it. For days there had been no medical treatment, except for desperate cases like my neighbor from Soest. This order had me worried.

I was always worried when I had to do something out of the ordinary. Mama had dinned it in to me that I should always do what everybody else was doing and never attract attention by doing any more or less. For twenty years, I obeyed her and long after Hitler was dead and gone I was terrified whenever I had to express an opinion or make myself conspicuous in any way.

With pounding heart I went down the corridor to the hospital commander's office. I knocked, entered, and saluted.

"Never mind that." He waved his hand as if to say that there was no further need of such formalities. He took some papers from his desk and said in an official tone, "Your record indicates a slight heart defect. You are unfit for active service and require treatment by a specialist. Preferably in Bad Nauheim."

Bad Nauheim was in the direction of Frankfurt and had not yet been occupied by the Americans.

"I've already made out your medical papers. And here are your marching orders. With them you shouldn't have any trouble." I looked at him incredulously.

204 | My Heart Defect

"Really," he said. "It's all set. Go to Bad Nauheim for treatment. And stay as long as you can." He put all my papers into an envelope and handed it to me. Then he said, "Good luck. I hope you make it. God bless you."

This meant that I would not have to go to the artillery post and, for some time at least, to the front. It wasn't until much later that I realized what a risk the doctor had taken in making out those papers.

I'd been examined by quite a few doctors, and none of them had ever diagnosed a heart defect; he had made that up just so as to send me to Bad Nauheim. To this day I have found no plausible explanation for his kindness to me. Why did he single me out? He could have done the same for the others, at least for some of them. He didn't. All the others who had been in quarantine with me were marched to the artillery post and shipped to the front.

The Hunting Lodge

Toward midday, while the soldiers capable of walking were being led in small groups from the hospital to the artillery post, a man in a green hunter's jacket appeared at the Ursuline convent. I'd seen him the day before and a few other times. He seemed to know his way around and shook hands with several of the nuns. He was a man in his middle forties, small and wiry, with the kind of face it's hard to remember.

When I left the ward with my bundle, intending to hit the road—trains had stopped running to Bad Nauheim and Frankfurt days before—he was standing in the entrance. He stopped me and began asking me questions. Where was I going? Was I very sick? Did I think I could get to Bad Nauheim without being stopped?

I was impatient, I wanted to get started so as to put a few miles between me and Fritzlar before dark. I felt too close for safety to the army post and the railroad station, where trains were still leaving for the front. I wanted to melt into the countryside as quickly as possible. I was about to go on, without waiting for him to stop talking. But then suddenly I pricked up my ears.

"My advice," said the hunter, patting me protectively on my shoulder, "is to keep away from the direct route via Alsfeld. If you go that way the M.P.'s are sure to get you. They're shipping everyone who can crawl to the front." This man must know the region well, I thought. Maybe I'd better listen to him and not be in such a hurry, since I didn't know the country at all, and I had no map. "Which way should I go, then?" I asked. "Can you tell me how to bypass the checkpoints?"

"You've come to the right man, comrade. At a time like this we're all comrades."

This was a strange and sudden familiarity. It seemed to me inappropriate to the circumstances. The hunter held his forehead as though giving my problem serious thought, and recommended a detour via Bad Wildungen, naming several byways. "That's your best bet."

Surprised at so much helpfulness in the bustle and confusion of the hospital evacuation, I thanked him profusely. He stopped me with a wave of the hand. "Don't mention it, comrade." Then he added, "It so happens that I'm going in that direction. I can take you part of the way if you like."

"I'd appreciate it," I said. "But what do you mean, 'take' me?"

"In a wagon. I've got a horse and wagon outside. Come on." With that he picked up my bundle and hurried out. Another soldier was standing in the driveway, evidently waiting for us. "He's coming too," said the hunter.

The carriage was at the door. There was room for all three of us on the driver's seat. The hunter took the reins and the horse started off.

We ran into the first check only a few minutes later, at the Fritzlar marketplace. A corporal examined our papers backward and forward, narrowed his eyes suspiciously, and asked, "How sick are you guys *really?*"

The hunter intervened. "Too sick to walk," he lied. "The

hospital has no vehicles left, so I'm taking them to Bad Wildungen."

The corporal seemed satisfied; our papers, after all, were in order. Before we could get out of the town, we were checked twice more. But after that there was no trouble.

"We won't take the main road," said the hunter. "Too dangerous. We wouldn't get far. We'll go around through the Elbebach Valley. It's a little longer, but I guarantee that we won't be stopped."

Why was this hunter going to so much trouble for us? I was getting suspicious. He must have some other purpose in mind than our safety. But what could it be?

After a while, the hunter said, "By the way, my name is Justus Mohl. I'm a game warden and I live in Heimarshausen. That's eight miles from Fritzlar. I grew up around here and I know the whole region like the back of my hand." He stopped and looked at us, as though expecting us to take up the conversation. But I had no desire to answer, and the other soldier seemed to feel the same way. The game warden was silenced for the moment, and it was so still that we could hear the twittering of the birds.

I leaned back as comfortably as I could on the hard seat and for a little while the war was far away. There was cannon fire in the distance, it sounded like the rumbling of a wide storm front. But I didn't let it bother me.

As we drove along, the other soldier told me that he too had been in the hospital with a contagious disease and had been discharged that same day. He really had heart trouble, or so he told me. He came from Neheim-Hüsten, where his father owned a furniture factory.

We must have been on the road for about an hour when we came to a small town by the name of Züschen. The game warden said very casually that it was past three o'clock, that we couldn't expect to go much farther that day, and that he knew of a good place to spend the night, a hunting lodge in the Heimarshausen Forest. Some women, whose husbands were off with the army, were living there. He was sure there'd be room for us and plenty to eat as well. He was the game warden in those parts.

The offer sounded attractive, but we couldn't make up our minds. One thing we didn't want was to be picked up by a military police patrol while spending the night in a place off our line of march. If that happened, we'd find ourselves at the front before we knew it.

"It's up to you," said the game warden, tightening the reins and urging the horse to a trot.

Ten minutes later we came to a crossroads. A signpost indicated that the left fork led to Bad Wildungen, which was on the route specified in our marching orders. "How about it?" he asked. "The hunting lodge is on the right. Are you coming? Yes or no?"

"How far is it?" I asked.

"Oh, about three miles."

Actually we had no choice.

"I'm with you," I said.

"So am I," said the other soldier.

About twenty minutes later we turned into a bumpy dirt road that climbed steadily to the edge of the forest. I was curious to see what we were getting into. It was clear to me by then what the game warden was doing. He had been meaning all along to lure us to this hunting lodge.

Though the hunting lodge was not very deep in the woods, we were almost there before we saw it. It was a good-sized three-story house with a large garden. Except for the opening at the gate the grounds were completely surrounded by a high wire-mesh fence.

Three women were standing at the gate. They gave us a friendly welcome and seemed to have been expecting us.

"Have you had a pleasant trip?" one of them asked.

And the second: "Are you very tired?"

And the third: "Do come in!"

The youngest of the three, who must have been in her early thirties, was slender, with sharp features and thin lips. Her smooth, ash-blond hair was parted in the middle and knotted loosely at the nape of her neck. The second looked to be about fifty. Neither thin nor fat, she had pleasant eyes, a kindly face, and white bobbed hair. The third might be going on sixty and seemed stiff in the joints.

We soon learned that the women, on hearing that the military hospital was being abandoned, had sent the game warden to bring back two soldiers for protection during the confusion that was to be expected during the next few weeks.

Justus Mohl had agreed to their plan, though he must have known what a risk he was taking—inciting us to desert and to hide at the hunting lodge. If he had been caught, he would almost certainly have been shot.

The three women were well aware of the danger of their action and took precautions. They kept saying, "Oh, we had nothing to do with it. It was Herr Mohl's idea."

Frau S., the young one with the sharp features and the bun, was in command. Frau B., the oldest, was her mother-in-law. Frau H., the one with the white hair and the friendly eyes, was no relation. The husbands of all three women were high-ranking officers; one was a general.

The talk soon came around to our stay. Without so much as mentioning the circumstances of our coming, Frau S. told us we could live in the house for as long as we liked, there was a bedroom available and they still had enough food. When the women went into the kitchen to make supper, Justus Mohl told us a little about the women's situation. Then he said, "Well, how about it? Are you staying or leaving? It's entirely up to you. No one's holding you. But I can tell you this: if you leave, the Americans will take you prisoner before you know it. So, which is it?"

I didn't take long to decide, I had no desire to be taken prisoner, though I knew the alternative meant risking our lives. If a Wehrmacht patrol caught us at the hunting lodge, they'd make short shrift of me. There was no reason to suppose they would overlook this particular house. If the Germans didn't get me and I fell into the hands of American combat troops, the same fate might befall me.

And yet there was something wrong with my reasoning. Common sense should have told me that I had no reason to fear the Americans, that their coming would set me free. But I was so afraid of being unmasked that I acted like a German deserter. It was as if the detested uniform covered my soul as well as my body. In my heart of hearts I hoped the war would be over soon, that I'd be freed from the mesh of lies I'd been living in, but my hope was overlaid by the fears of a German soldier. My behavior in those weeks was motivated on the one hand by cowardice and on the other by the Jewish aptitude for adjusting to any situation, however humiliating, when survival is at stake.

The three women were convinced that the front would soon be rolling over them. They were terrified, but that didn't stop them from mouthing phrases about "fighting to the last ditch" and "holding on to the bitter end." Maybe they thought they owed that to their husbands. Their special dread was that during the period of disorder between the withdrawal of the German troops and the arrival of the Allies, hundreds of thousands of Russian and Polish forced laborers would break out of their camps. But for all their fears, they were without consciousness of guilt. They felt they were still in the right and always had been. But by the time all this had become fully clear to me, I, the son of Moissey Rabizanovich and Olga Sudakovich, I who had yearned for the day when the Americans or the Russians, I didn't much care which, would put an end to the Nazi nightmare, had been promoted to the rank of bodyguard to three women each one of whom would have sent me to the gas chambers without batting an eyelash if they had known my secret.

Frau S., who gave the orders in the house, had a strong sense of the practical. During the next week, when nothing happened that would require our services as protectors, she kept us busy from morning to night, for the other soldier had also decided to stay. Our day started with half an hour's hike to the baker's in Heimarshausen for bread and rolls and to a farm for fresh milk. We sawed and chopped wood, moved furniture, mended the fence, and worked in the garden. And there was always something in the house that needed repairing.

But then things began to happen. For two days the defeated German troops poured through the valley and the forest. They were tired of fighting, they knew the end was near, and they had no desire to die like heroes in the last hour. There was fear and despair in their faces, many limped, others were swathed in bandages. All had abandoned their weapons. On the road down below us an unbroken line of vehicles was moving northward, all packed full of men in uniform.

When the German troops were all gone except for a few isolated stragglers, the game warden said, "You'll have to get rid of your uniforms now, or the Americans will pick you up."

We knew he was right. "Where are we going to find civilian clothes?" I asked him.

"No problem. I've taken care of that. Come."

He led us down to the front hallway. There lay two pairs of old trousers and two ragged jackets.

"Quick," he said. "You don't want to be seen changing."

So I turned myself back into a civilian, a pretty bedraggled one, to be sure, for the trousers were too long, I had to turn up the legs; the jacket was a size too big and the sweaty lining was torn.

The next morning at daybreak Mohl came for us. We put our uniforms and papers in a big box and carried them out to the woods. He expected the Americans to be there in a few hours. That's why he was in such a hurry.

Unbeknownst to the others, I had put aside my foreigner's passport, which I had always carried with me in the barracks and at the hospital. And now I kept it.

We buried the box at the foot of a big tree, covered the

hole with branches and leaves, and marked a few of the trees roundabout. When we got back an hour later, the three women were busy burying their money and jewelry in different parts of the garden, in among the onions and carrots, the chives and celery sprouts.

Is This Liberation?

In fear and trepidation we looked down the dirt road leading out to the highway. Who would come first, the Poles from one of the many labor camps in the region, or the Americans? Whoever it was, would they storm the house, would they shoot, or would they just quietly come in?

The three women heard on the radio that the Germans were retreating on all fronts. A disaster, a misfortune, they called it. Naturally I was delighted; every German defeat or withdrawal was ground for hope.

Suddenly shots were heard. The sound came from the woods about a mile away on the other side of the highway. Tanks came racing down the highway, firing into the woods. I could distinctly see the muzzle flashes. Shots were returned from the woods. They sounded like the snapping of a whip. This went on for fifteen or twenty minutes. Then silence, except for an isolated shot now and then.

And then at last they came! Two jeeps came bouncing over the dirt road, leaving a wide trail of dust behind them.

Much as I dreaded this first meeting with American combat troops, I was glad it was them rather than liberated Poles.

As we had decided beforehand, we all went outside, the three women and we two demobilized soldiers, the son of the furniture manufacturer bringing up the rear. Justus Mohl had preferred to await the Americans at home with his wife in Heimarshausen.

The gate was wide open, but the two jeeps didn't drive in. They stopped at some distance from the gate. Six soldiers, fully armed, their tommy guns drawn, jumped out. Only the two black drivers stayed in the jeeps and kept their motors running. Slowly, darting nervous glances in all directions as though expecting to be attacked, the six approached the gate. At some thirty yards from us they stopped and leveled their guns at us.

"Hands up!" one of them shouted. We raised our arms.

Another with three stripes on his sleeve waved his gun at me and barked, "Come here, you!"

I wasn't surprised. Whom else was the sergeant to call? The son of the furniture manufacturer? Ever since we'd known each other he had let me take the lead. It was only logical, therefore, that the American pointed at me. Hypnotized, I stared into the muzzle of the tommy gun the sergeant was waving at me. "Come on!" he shouted again.

Slowly, with upraised arms, I walked toward the American soldiers.

*

Do you remember, Mama, how often, in our little living room in the back building on Kaiserhofstrasse, we sat dreaming of when and how an end would be put to our deadly fears, how we wondered whether it would be the Russians, Americans, or the British who came to Frankfurt first, to bring us back to life? Do you remember the way Alex would act out the scene of our liberation? In one version, they crash through the front gate in a tank, all guns ablaze; they smash the heavy doors because they are in too much of a hurry to unlatch them, the tank would come rolling into the back court where Petri the cheese merchant kept his handcarts and reduce them all to kindling with a quick swiveling movement. Out of sheer playfulness. Then the turret would open; a Russian, British, or American helmet would appear, and a loud voice would cry, "Hey, you people up there, come on out! There's nothing to be afraid of now. No more Nazis! So come on out! Nothing can happen to you now!"

A beautiful vision. But you were against it, Mama. You didn't want any tanks barging into the yard because of the horrible jangling of the treads, not to mention the shooting. Making kindling of Petri's carts didn't appeal to you either. If it had been up to you, several soldiers would rush into the yard, without shooting, if possible, and one, who had already been told where to find us, would climb the stairs of the back building. He'd knock at the door, once, twice, and call out: "Open up. What are you hiding for?" Alex disagreed. If they came on foot, and one of them ran up the stairs, all right, but it wouldn't do for him to knock politely and ask if we were at home. What kind of liberation would that be? No! No! It had to be like this: Before we could open the door, he would kick it in with his heavy boots and yell, "You're free! Go where you like! Out with you!" And whoever he was, a Russian Ivan, a French Poilu, a British Tommy, or an American G.I., we'd squeeze the wind out of him with our hugging, drown him in our tears, smother him with our kisses.

And we'd be so moved at the thought of this day of liberation and our hope of living to see it that real tears would come to our eyes.

Mama, you knew your heart wouldn't hold out that long; you didn't kid yourself; you had the courage to face the truth, but you joined in our dreams of liberation just the same. "Even if I don't live to see it," you'd say, "I can dream about it at least." And you'd try to smile.

Alex never grew tired of dreaming up more and more

liberation scenes. In my favorite, all the other occupants of our house, everybody on the whole street in fact, would run away from the Americans or Russians. But we'd stay right where we were. And when they came, we'd run out into the street and yell, "We're saved! We're free!"

And the astonished soldiers would ask: "Why are you saved? Who are you?"

And we'd say: "We're Jews."

They'd ask again: "What are you?"

And we'd shout: "We're Jews!"

"You'll have to speak louder!" they'd order.

And we'd shout again. "We are Jews."

"Louder still!"

And we'd cup our hands around our mouths and shout in all directions until we were hoarse:

"We're Jews! We're Jews! We're saved!"

And we'd dance in the street, Mama, Papa, Paula, Alex, and I, we'd dance till we dropped with exhaustion.

*

Now the liberators had come.

But what kind of liberation was this? Here was a tommy gun aimed at my belly and the man holding it meant business. He didn't give a good goddamn whether I was a Jew or a Holy Roller—he had come as a victor, and we were the vanquished, including me. Call this a liberation? All the dreams of our little family had been spun in vain. No hugs, no kisses, no tears of joy, no shouting, no dancing. And I'd have to go right on lying, right on trembling.

If anyone had ever told me the liberation would be like this, I'd have called him a liar or a fool. If I'd tried to think up ten thousand possibilities, this scene outside the hunting lodge in Heimarshausen would not have been one of them.

Slowly, with my hands up, I approached the American soldiers. I remember one of them well. He was a head shorter than the others and he had a harelip. He jiggled his tommy gun menacingly. I was afraid he'd pull the trigger by mistake.

"Are you a German soldier?" the sergeant asked.

"No." I pulled my passport out of my jacket.

"What's that?"

"A foreigner's passport," I said in English. "I am not a German." I pointed to the French title on the cover: *Passeport pour étrangers.*

Luckily for me, the American seemed to understand that much French. "Stateless" had him baffled, but when I told him my parents had come from Russia, he seemed satisfied.

Then he asked about the other soldier. He seemed satisfied when I told him the man was a civilian and had a certificate showing that he had heart trouble and was unfit for military service.

"Nobody else in the house?" the American asked.

"No."

Another American soldier frisked me and the other German soldier for weapons. Then the sergeant ordered one of his men to stay outside and guard the other Germans while I led him and the rest of the squad into the house. They searched one room after another. I had to go ahead, opening every drawer and cupboard. The one with the harelip was the most thorough.

"No arms in the house?" one of them asked.

"No," I said.

We got to the kitchen.

"No schnapps?"

I went into the living room, brought out an opened bottle of cognac and a full bottle of wine, and handed them over.

"Is that all?"

I shrugged. "I think so."

"Now the ground floor," the sergeant ordered.

Downstairs, next to the garage, there were additional rooms to which I had never been admitted. I had to open up and wait outside, while they searched them. I was kind of worried, because after a week with those women I wouldn't have put anything past them. But there was nothing in the room but old junk. I began to breathe easy. We filed out. But one of the soldiers stayed behind and poked around in the corners.

Suddenly he let out a whistle and I turned around in a fright. He had discovered a door leading into a tiny little room. In the beam of his flashlight, I saw that the place looked like an air shaft and was empty. But the soldier wasn't satisfied. He knew all about these supposedly empty rooms. He tapped the walls with his gun butt and pounded the floor with his boots. The floor rang hollow. It became obvious that the floor was covered only with a wooden plank. The American pried up some of the boards, which were not nailed down. I was paralyzed with terror at what I saw in the beam of a flashlight: a whole storeroom full of provisions; crates, cans and jars full of food, a case of wine and another of cognac. The soldier jumped down into the storeroom and handed up all the liquor and a good part of the food. Another grabbed me by the coat collar and furiously pushed my head against the iron doorframe several times.

"No schnapps, eh?" he bellowed. "No schnapps, the man says!"

He was in a rage. He thought I'd known about the liquor all along. He jabbed his knee into my belly and banged my head against the doorframe again. Probably to discourage me from defending myself, the little one kept his tommy gun leveled at me and kicked me repeatedly in the shins. It hurt like hell.

He's going to kill me, I thought, and collapsed. He stopped kicking me, growled "Fuckin' kraut!" and pushed me down on the ground. The little one poked me in the kidneys with his toe and I let out a scream. Then they left and forgot all about me.

Aching in my head and my back, I staggered out past the three women and the son of the furniture manufacturer, who were standing in the open doorway of the garage. They had witnessed the scene.

The general's wife, the one with the white hair, took me by the arm and asked, "Can I help you? Are you hurt?"

Blood was dripping from my nose. I wiped it off with the back of my hand. One of the soldiers must have hit me with his gun butt in the coccyx. That was where it hurt most. I dragged myself to the stairs. Then I passed out.

When I came to, I was lying on the living room sofa. Someone had taken off my shoes and thrown a blanket over me. Frau S. was looking after me. She brought me a glass of water and laid a cold damp cloth on my head. The Americans had driven away.

I stared at the ceiling. Little by little, I remembered what had happened. A pretty mess! Had I miraculously escaped discovery and death more times than I could count only to be massacred by my liberators because three women had hidden their hoard of food and liquor?

I held my aching head in my hands, blinked at the sunlight, and resolved to get out of that hunting lodge as soon as I possibly could.

The Ax Under My Pillow

First it was only two of them. The two Poles circled the house, examining it from all sides. Then they came in, made sure there were no American soldiers around, and asked for food. Frau S. gave them sausage, bread, and two jars of canned food. That seemed to satisfy them and they left. But we had good reason to be anxious. Their curiosity had been too obvious, it was plain they had been reconnoitering. We knew they'd be back—and not alone next time. We fortified the house as best we could, barricaded the doors, and secured the shutters on the ground floor. My fellow soldier and I were moved from our bedroom to a room downstairs near the front door. Then Frau S. gave each of us an ax and told us to keep them under our pillows to defend ourselves with if the Poles came during the night.

Imagine giving *me* an ax to bash someone's head in with! Only a man with iron nerves can sleep with an ax under his pillow. Sure I was afraid the Poles might come during the night, but what scared me a damn sight more was the thought of defending myself with an ax. I'd rather have let myself be killed with an ax than use one on someone else.

I reached under my pillow to feel the ax blade. Not so very sharp, that was a relief, and plenty of nicks, like a plain ordinary ax that you chop wood with.

Then the ax handle began digging into my shoulders. When I turned my head to the left, the blunt end of the ax head pressed against my ear and the handle dug into my carotid. The only way to avoid the ax completely was to lie so close to the edge of the bed that I almost fell out. That wasn't very comfortable either.

Suddenly it occurred to me that this same blade that lay between pillow and mattress two inches away from my neck might be used to sever my head from my neck. Why not?

My whole body was bathed in sweat.

I couldn't stand it any longer. I pulled the ax out from under my pillow and laid it down on the floor. That calmed me a little. Exhausted and overtired, I fell into a restless half sleep, but started up at the slightest sound. Each time I thought the Poles must be coming.

The ax gave me no peace. It began to grow. It grew and grew, and turned into an enormous butcher's cleaver. Then the handle grew, and the cleaver became an executioner's ax. Two arms tattooed from top to bottom were holding the handle. The owner of the tattooed arms stood firmly planted at the foot end of the bed. He was wearing a pointed hood like a Ku Klux Klansman. The polished blade stood out against the dark background. This was a very special kind of executioner's ax, it kept making grimaces and changing its shape in waves as though it lay at the bottom of a clear, gently moving pool of water.

Then it was morning. The Poles had not come.

I've often thought of Heimarshausen and all that happened there. What I remember most vividly is the night I spent with the ax. I keep wondering why I didn't throw it away.

I wanted to throw it away, but my arm was numb, as though it had fallen asleep, my hand was physically incapable of grabbing the ax handle. It was as if I were paralyzed. I had often had that feeling of paralysis in the past, starting in my school days. It has been with me all my life. It almost drove me to despair; I cursed it but I couldn't get rid of it.

Once on the street a boy of my own age started beating up Alex. I wasn't afraid of him; I grabbed him by the arm, I wanted to hit him—but I couldn't. Sometimes in a discussion group I'd think I had something important to say and raise my hand; I'd stand up—but then I couldn't open my mouth. There was one time when I wanted to go up to a woman and propose to her, I knew she was expecting it—and no power on earth could have got a word out of me.

I think I know where this paralysis began: in the back building of No. 12 Kaiserhofstrasse. That's where the seed was sown. Papa, Paula, Alex, and I—we were all condemned to passivity. By Mama. For fear we'd make a mistake, for fear we'd give ourselves away, she thought and acted for the whole family. She infected me with her fear. And that's where my paralysis came from. It prevented me from stepping up to the Americans and saying, "I'm a Jew!" And it also prevented me from throwing that ax out of the window in a wide arc.

Late that morning the Poles came. Eight of them, armed with rifles, knives, and iron bars. From the window we saw them coming out of the woods and taking up positions. Early that morning we had sensibly put our axes back where they belonged, in the woodshed.

A few minutes later one of the Poles knocked on the door and shouted: "Open!" While I went out to open the front door, the others stayed in the large room on the ground floor.

Two rifles were pointed at me. One of the Poles poked the barrel of his gun into my chest and pushed me back to the wall. "Where other people?" he asked in broken German.

"In the living room," I answered.

"Go first."

I obeyed his orders and led the way. Now the gun barrel was pressed into my back.

We went into the living room where the others were standing.

"Everybody in toilet!" the Pole commanded. They pushed us into the bathroom and locked the door. It was a small room and there were five of us. There was no way of avoiding physical contact with the women. Frau B. sat on the toilet seat, rubbing her forehead with cologne, or holding her head in her hands and moaning, "Will we ever get out of here alive?"

The rest of us stood there trembling, asking ourselves the same question. Quite superfluously one of the Poles called in through the locked door: "Anybody come out get shot!"

They ransacked the house. Thumping, rumbling, and crashing could be heard on all sides. They slammed doors, dragged trunks and boxes down steps and along corridors.

In the midst of it two Poles came into the bathroom and seized the women's wristwatches, rings, and any other jewelry they had not buried. I had to let them take the beautiful wristwatch Mimi had given me for my birthday.

The whole raid took about three-quarters of an hour. Then there was silence. They were gone.

We waited another little while before breaking down the door. The rooms themselves and the furniture were not badly damaged, but all valuables were gone—clocks, silverware, candlesticks. The Poles had also made off with boots, shoes, bedsheets, and tablecloths.

The women crept from room to room, looking into empty drawers and cupboards, weeping and wailing and cursing the Polish barbarians.

Those women had had their share of trouble, but I couldn't feel sorry for them. Even if we were in the same boat for the moment, I couldn't regard them as companions in suffering. Our forced stay together between bathtub and toilet bowl had forged no ties of solidarity. They had disliked me from the start and the feeling was mutual.

All the women at the hunting lodge distrusted me, and so did the other soldier. They kept a close watch on everything I did. They stopped talking when I passed by and I often heard them whispering behind closed doors. And after a while, when Frau S. had an order to give me, she'd do it indirectly through the other soldier.

They had seen me talking with the American sergeant and showing him my passport. That had puzzled them and added to their distrust.

Some time after the Americans had beaten me up, Frau S. asked me: "What were those papers you showed them?"

"A foreigner's passport."

"Aren't you German?"

"No."

"What then?"

"Stateless."

"Then why were you in the army?"

"Your guess is as good as mine."

"I don't understand."

"Neither do I."

There the conversation had ended. I could feel it hadn't helped matters.

I racked my brains. How was I to get away from that hunting lodge? But once you had a hiding place at a time like that, you didn't leave it. Where else could I go?

Confide in the Americans? Out of the question. They wouldn't have believed my story. It was too incredible. I couldn't go home to Frankfurt. I'd have been picked up on the road. Every time I looked out at the highway, I'd see American trucks loaded with German soldiers and civilians. On their way to some prison camp, no doubt. That didn't appeal to me at all.

What a spot I was in! I had been freed of my fear of being

recognized as a Jew. But another fear had taken its place: the fear of being exposed as a deserter.

I was feeling more and more uneasy. My situation was desperate and I could think of no way out. So I stayed on at the hunting lodge, supposedly to protect these women against American or Polish looters, and I lived in fear of having my skull bashed in.

I wouldn't have admitted it even to myself, but the hunting lodge gave me a certain sense of security and that's why I never thought seriously of escaping. In spite of all my fears, this house was a den, a nest. A nasty sort of den, but it provided warmth; a nest of barbed wire, but it provided shelter. Much as I disliked my companions, we had one thing in common: our fears. The place offered security. In spite of everything.

The Polish raid was reported to the American Occupation authorities. After that patrols came by several times a day to check. Actually, it wasn't so much our welfare that interested them as our liquor supply, which Justus Mohl kept replenishing. That was easy enough for him. The local population had looted the stores of the Fritzlar army post and had got their hands on a supply train that had been abandoned between Kassel and Fritzlar. Everybody seemed to have a few bottles of schnapps. The barter trade flourished, and who wouldn't have been glad to trade a bottle or two of liquor for a hare or a haunch of venison offered them by the game warden? Thus Mohl could always renew the dwindling alcohol supply.

The Americans appreciated our liquor, and they enjoyed the cultivated atmosphere they found at the hunting lodge; they felt flattered when the general's wife or Frau S. trotted out her school English for their benefit.

The women found no difficulty in making friends with their enemies of the day before. The enemy now was Communism, and this was an enemy they could share with their new friends. Suddenly the whole war with the Americans, British, and French ceased to be anything more than a tragic misunderstanding. The only real enemy was the Russians, the Communists.

It was soon bruited about in the surrounding villages that the Americans were frequent visitors at the hunting lodge, and in fact for the present we had nothing to fear from looters. Peasants began bringing good things to eat and asking us to persuade "our American friends" to cancel some annoying regulation, to return some confiscated vehicle, or merely to barter cigarettes for butter and eggs.

The C.O.

One morning a jeep came driving up the road. Lots of jeeps had appeared in the last few days. But this time the Americans hadn't come for liquor or to check us out; they had come for me.

I wasn't terribly upset. I knew I couldn't go on hiding forever. "Where are we going?" was all I asked them.

"The C.O. wants to see you." C.O. stood for commanding officer. I'd learned that much by then.

The Americans had installed their command post at Schloss Garvensburg, ten minutes' drive from the hunting lodge.

I had to wait in the lobby. A soldier stayed with me. The Occupation troops were doing their best to keep some sort of local government going, and there were streams of German civilians coming and going. Finally I was called in. The C.O., a lieutenant as it happened, had set up his office in the castle library, a large room with leather-upholstered chairs and an enormous ornate desk. He asked me to sit down across the desk from him.

I could see that the officer was eying me strangely, as if he suspected me of God knew what. He was young, maybe twenty-five, held the rank of lieutenant, and was rather small for such a big desk. With his black hair, dark eyes, and narrow face, I almost thought he might be Jewish. But not really; he was too spruce and military looking.

At his side sat two noncoms. One interpreted, the other took notes.

I was calm. I wasn't afraid any more. I waited with resignation for the American to tell me I had been identified as a former German soldier and was to be sent off to a prison camp.

But I was in for one more surprise. With no attempt at tactical subtlety, the American informed me that I was suspected of having been a spy in the service of the Russians. If the suspicion were confirmed, I'd be sent right back where I belonged; the American-occupied zone was no place for eastern spies.

It took me a moment to catch on. Me a Russian spy! What gave them that idea? My stateless passport! That was it —my passport. Either it had aroused the suspicion of the sergeant who had first checked it, or one of the women had denounced me to the Americans for the same reason.

Pleadingly, stressing every word, I said, "I am not a spy, Lieutenant! I have never been a spy!"

"You'll have to prove it. For the present we suspect you of being one." The noncom translated it all.

"You could suspect everybody."

"We don't suspect everybody. We suspect you."

"Have you reasons for suspecting me?" I asked.

"Of course we have reasons. We wouldn't have brought you here if we hadn't."

"What are these reasons?"

That made him angry. "I ask the questions here. All right. Where are you from? How did you get here?"

This was the last, in fact the best chance to tell the truth; to tell them who I was and what adventures had brought me to the hunting lodge. But I kept on lying, obsessed by the thought that I must not tell the commanding officer that I had worn the uniform of a German soldier, I told him I had lived in Frankfurt until a few weeks before, and had fled when they wanted to put me in the army.

"I don't believe you," said the lieutenant. "They don't take foreigners in the army, and according to your passport you're a foreigner."

I assured him that it was nevertheless true, and that if he made inquiries in Frankfurt he'd find out that I had been born there and had lived there all my life. The interpreter translated and the lieutenant listened attentively. He asked for another look at my passport and leafed through it. I had the feeling that he was beginning to believe me.

"We'll make inquiries in Frankfurt," he said. "In the meantime, you are not to move from your present address." With that he dismissed me and I was driven back to the hunting lodge.

The ladies were surprised to see me back. It was plain that they had already written me off. Frau S. made no attempt to conceal her disappointment. "What did they want of you at headquarters?" she asked.

"I'm not allowed to say," I replied, and turned away. Let her burst with curiosity. As likely as not, the whole business had been her doing.

The hostility between me and the others got worse and worse. To avoid spending the whole day with them, I took to going to Heimarshausen and helping the peasant women with their farmwork. Their husbands were all in the army and those who were still alive hadn't come home yet. I showed myself less and less at the hunting lodge, which didn't break anyone's heart. Contrary to the American lieutenant's orders, I often spent the night at Justus Mohl's house.

Mohl's wife, who had no children of her own, treated me

like a son, washed my clothes, darned my socks, and asked me what I'd like to eat. She made up a bed for me on the living room couch. She must have been in her late forties, about the same age as her husband and, like most country women of that age, had long been beyond good and evil. She was short and squat, with piano legs in black woolen stockings, and no waist. She waddled when she walked. But when she laughed, which she did rarely, because Justus never had a kind word for her, you could see that she must have been beautiful once. Aside from that, nothing remained of her youth but two little gold earrings with red stones—which she never took off—and a withered wedding garland in a moldy cardboard box with a pink silk ribbon round it, which I once discovered in among a mass of spiderwebs and litter while exploring the attic.

I was very fond of her. She was good and kind, generous even to Justus, though he made her very unhappy. One girl friend wasn't enough for him, he needed two, to make him feel virile, one in the next village, who was said to be slightly feebleminded, and a farm woman in Heimarshausen, whose husband had been killed at the beginning of the war.

I soon won Frau Mohl's confidence and she told me her troubles. She had no one else to confide in and she poured out her heart.

One day a distant relative of Mohl's came back from Holland, where she had served as a Wehrmacht auxiliary. She'd been arrested by the Allied troops, but they hadn't held her for long. She had stayed at the game warden's house before, and now she moved back into the same little room. Frau Mohl wasn't at all happy about it. "It'll be the same old circus all over again," she said sadly. Her name was Gerdi. She was a few years older than I was and at least an inch taller. With her bony frame, her big angular face and her prominent teeth that were much in evidence, she somehow reminded me of a farm horse. Her dark stringy hair fell almost to her shoulders. Her hands were large and sinewy; she was as strong as an ox.

She brought life into the house. Every evening she wanted

to make a party of it. The game warden brought bottle after bottle of wine and schnapps from the cellar; he couldn't resist Gerdi. When she threw her arm round him and rubbed her bony cheek against his, every bit of willpower seeped away and he'd run down for one more bottle. In return, he had the privilege, when his wife wasn't in the room, of grabbing her thigh at the very top so that the back of his hand rubbed her stomach, and squeezing so hard that she squeaked with pleasure and pain.

Frau Mohl kept her eye on the two of them. If she came back from the kitchen a little too soon, Gerdi would pretend to be indignant and slap Mohl on the back of his hand. Frau Mohl would never say anything more than a reproachful "Oh, Justus!" But she was very unhappy. One day she took me aside and suggested that I pay a little attention to Gerdi. She knew I knew why she was asking me, and she was terribly embarrassed. "Of course you don't have to," she said. "But you're both unattached. Would you like me to speak to her?"

"Good God, no. I can do that myself."

"I'm sorry," she said. "I only thought . . ."

Her recommendation was unnecessary. I liked Gerdi, not so much for her figure as for her way of laughing, her free and easy manner, and her obvious man-hunger. But I had a feeling that I wasn't really her type and that she probably wanted a big strong man with a grip like a vise. I didn't answer to that description, and that made me sad.

Once or twice the other soldier joined us at our revels. To my annoyance, Gerdi took an unmistakable liking to him, though he still looked very pale. Luckily he was even more inhibited that I was and so awkward in his approaches that she soon lost interest in him and finally turned to me. It was past midnight when the party broke up. Before going to her room, Gerdi gave me a long eloquent look.

To reach Gerdi's room I had to go through the hall and down a short flight of stairs which led directly to her room. The only door was at the top of the stairs and the upper half of it was glassed. When I thought Justus and his wife must have fallen asleep, I got up, pulled my trousers on, and crept quietly out of the living room. Gerdi was expecting me. The door was ajar, and she had left her bedside lamp on to light the stairs.

I had my clothes off in no time and slipped under the covers. Gerdi welcomed me with a stormy embrace. What a wonderful smell, like fresh milk and silage. Gerdi was in a hurry, she'd waited long enough, she wanted no preludes, no beating about the bush.

Suddenly I gave a start and let Gerdi go. I had heard steps and the creaking of a door.

"Gerdi!" I whispered, startled. "Somebody's there."

"Really? Oh, that must be Justus, the horny old goat," she answered none too quietly.

"But he can look down and see us." The bed was right at the foot of the stairs and there was a direct view through the glass pane in the door. As I looked up, I thought I could see a head behind the glass.

"He's up there watching us," I whispered. "I'm sure."

"That's just like him. But who cares!" Gerdi didn't seem to mind at all.

"At least put the light out," I pleaded.

"Why?" She shot back, "Does it bother you?"

"Yes, he can see everything we do."

She laughed. "Let him watch. It gives me a kick." And after a pause: "That way he'll get something out of it too." She pulled me close again. Then suddenly she stopped moving. "What's the matter?" she gasped. "You're not there any more." That was God's truth. The thought of somebody watching us had been too much for me. The spirit was willing but the flesh had lain down on the job.

"I'm sorry, Gerdi," I stammered, "but I can't do it if he's up there watching."

"Then we'll just send him to bed."

"Never mind. I think it's too late now."

"Oh, come on. We don't want to stop halfway, do we? Take your time. Or don't you like me?"

"I like you very much, Gerdi."

"Then go ahead."

"No. It won't work tonight. I know myself."

"Christ, you're weird! If I'd only known!" She rolled over on the other side, turning her back on me.

I took her by the arm. "Forgive me, Gerdi, I really can't help it."

"Leave me alone!" She was disappointed and hurt. I pulled on my trousers, gave Gerdi, who had buried her head in her pillow, a kiss on her bare shoulder, and crept up to bed. I didn't sleep well that night.

After that Gerdi avoided me, and I kept out of her way. We hardly said a word to each other. Then came Sunday. After lunch Justus Mohl and his wife went out to visit some neighbors. Gerdi and I were alone in the house. She put a record on the gramophone and sat down in the living room. When I sat down beside her and tried to get affectionate, she rebuffed me. "Don't bother," she said. "I've got no use for limp goods. I know other men who can do it right."

She shouldn't have said that. In a rage I knocked a bun she was nibbling out of her hand, pushed her down on the couch with all my might, and flung myself on top of her. We slid off the narrow couch and lay on the wooden floor.

I was horrified at my loss of control; In a moment I'd pulled myself together and was about to let her go. But she was strangely calm; she didn't resist at all and made no move to get up. On the contrary, she did her best, despite the hardness of the floor, to find the right position under me. Her legs spread of their own accord. We melted into each other. And again that bewitching smell. But I didn't just smell her, I felt her and tasted her, saw and heard her. With a deep grunting sound she sank her teeth so firmly into my shoulder that days later I could still see the livid mark in the mirror.

That same night Gerdi fell sick, she had a high fever and pains in the small of her back. I sat by her bedside, putting cold compresses on her forehead, and held her hand. I could feel how thankful she was to have someone caring for her. The next day the doctor came from Züschen and diagnosed inflammation of the kidneys. Soon after his visit I was called back to the American command post.

Papa Was Standing at the Window

The officer received me with a friendly smile and even held out his hand. "I have good news from Frankfurt. Your statements have been confirmed."

I gave a sigh of relief. "So I'm not under suspicion any more?"

"No, you're not under suspicion any more."

We sat down on a sofa, and the officer said, "Just tell me one thing. Why are you stateless?"

"That would be hard to explain."

"You could try."

The time had come. I took a deep breath—I felt as though I were pulling a bowstring with my last strength before releasing the arrow.

"I'm a Jew."

The American stood up, took a few steps to the desk, came back, stopped in front of me, and stared at me in silence.

"Maybe you don't believe me? I really am a Jew."

"I believe you."

"We lived in Frankfurt. In hiding, no, illegally, no, that's not right either. Oh, it's hard to explain."

The American officer took me by the arms and shook me. "To me you want to explain? What is there to explain? It's a miracle. God protected you!"

"Yes, me and my family."

"I'm Jewish myself." His English lapsed and he went on in a mixture of German and Yiddish. "My father and mother are both from around Lodz. They went to the U.S. in 1921. I was born on shipboard. We live in Boston." He sat down beside me and put his arm over my shoulder. "But how did you manage it? How did you come through?"

"How? I often wonder myself."

"You must tell me about it. Are you Orthodox?"

"No."

"Good. Because today is *Shabbes.*" He held out his cigarette case, gave me a light, and lit up himself.

"Do you drink?"

"Nothing I like better."

He went out and came back with a bottle of whiskey and two glasses. He filled the glasses, raised his, and said: *"L'chayim!"*

"L'chayim!"

A little later a German servant brought us coffee and pastry.

Then I told him the story of the Senger family, haltingly and incompletely. Gradually layer after layer unfolded.

When I had finished, the lieutenant was silent. After a while, he asked, "Is there anything I can do to help you?"

"I'd like to go back to my family in Frankfurt. Could you give me a pass to get me through?"

"Is that all?"

"That's all. I just want to go home."

A day later I left the hunting lodge. I was thoroughly sick of its occupants, the three officers' wives, and the son of the furniture manufacturer. I said goodbye to Justus Mohl, to his wife, for whom I felt very sorry and who for a few weeks had been a good mother to me, and to poor sick, horse-faced Gerdi, with whom it hadn't come off the first time but had come off fine the second time, and who for one short hour had made me forget the hunting lodge and everyone in it.

In my pocket I had a pass assuring me of safe conduct to Frankfurt. That was at the end of April 1945.

On May 8, the day of the German capitulation, I arrived in Frankfurt. I came to the Main not far from the demolished iron footbridge. All the bridges connecting Frankfurt with Sachsenhausen had been blown up by the retreating German troops.

I crossed on a big flat-bottomed rowboat that was being used as an emergency ferry. On the Frankfurt shore I saw the shattered Römer and the heavily damaged Kaiserdom. Halfway across the river the boat began to rock because two men standing in the middle with their bicycles lost their balance. A bicycle fell on my knee and almost knocked me overboard. Only a skillful maneuver on the part of the ferryman saved me. My left arm was already in the water.

With a wet jacket and a beating heart, I ran through a field of ruins and over mountains of rubble. I passed the demolished Hauptwache and headed for Opernplatz. The last remaining houses of the old city were charred or in ruins, and large parts of the inner city just weren't there any more.

The closer I came to Kaiserhofstrasse, the more my knees wobbled. I slowed down. There was Kleinböhl's dairy, there was Weinschrod's fruit store, and there on the corner was Petri's cheese emporium. I looked down the street, wondering if I'd see No. 12, with the gas lamp in front of it. Thank God, the gas lamp was still there, and so was the house. I wondered if Papa and Paula would be home. Papa was sure to be. I had a hunch he'd be standing at the window when I came into the back court, that he'd be looking down at the entrance, waiting for Alex and me.

I turned in at the gate, went through the dark passage, and looked up. There stood Papa at the window, looking down, staring at the archway that I had just passed through. He looked as if he'd been standing like that for weeks and months, day and night, waiting for Alex and me.